T0197298

In Christ Jesus

In Christ Jesus

TELL MY PEOPLE WHO THEY ARE

JEAN S. JONES

IN CHRIST JESUS
TELL MY PEOPLE WHO THEY ARE

Copyright © 2018 Jean S. Jones.

All rights reserved. No part of this book may be used or reproduced by any means, graphic, electronic, or mechanical, including photocopying, recording, taping or by any information storage retrieval system without the written permission of the author except in the case of brief quotations embodied in critical articles and reviews.

The views expressed in this work are solely those of the author and do not necessarily reflect the views of the publisher, and the publisher hereby disclaims any responsibility for them.

Scripture quotations marked KJV are from the Holy Bible, King James Version (Authorized Version). First published in 1611. Quoted from the KJV Classic Reference Bible, Copyright © 1983 by The Zondervan Corporation.

Scripture quotations marked NLT are taken from the Holy Bible, New Living Translation, copyright © 1996, 2004, 2007. Used by permission of Tyndale House Publishers, Inc. Carol Stream, Illinois 60188. All rights reserved. Website

Scripture quotations marked AMP are from The Amplified Bible, Old Testament copyright © 1965, 1987 by the Zondervan Corporation. The Amplified Bible, New Testament copyright © 1954, 1958, 1987 by The Lockman Foundation. Used by permission. All rights reserved.

iUniverse books may be ordered through booksellers or by contacting:

iUniverse
1663 Liberty Drive
Bloomington, IN 47403
www.iuniverse.com
1-800-Authors (1-800-288-4677)

Because of the dynamic nature of the Internet, any web addresses or links contained in this book may have changed since publication and may no longer be valid. The views expressed in this work are solely those of the author and do not necessarily reflect the views of the publisher, and the publisher hereby disclaims any responsibility for them.

Any people depicted in stock imagery provided by Getty Images are models, and such images are being used for illustrative purposes only. Certain stock imagery © Getty Images.

ISBN: 978-1-5320-5920-9 (sc)
ISBN: 978-1-5320-5921-6 (e)

Library of Congress Control Number: 2018911942

Print information available on the last page.

iUniverse rev. date: 10/17/2018

CONTENTS

INTRODUCTION

When we made the decision to accept Jesus as our Savior, we were "born again" into His kingdom. We were also given the gift of the Holy Spirit, spiritual gifts to be used to edify, build up or encourage our brothers and sisters who are Christians, and special weapons to help us war against our enemy the Devil. God's promises had already been made available to us through the death of His Son, Jesus Christ.

Now that we are in Christ Jesus, we have the opportunity to truly know and reconnect with God who has loved us since the beginning of time. Before we came to Jesus, God being a holy God, could not tolerate our sins. Because Jesus sacrificed his life for us over two thousand years ago by dying for our sins on the cross, the blood he shed covers our sins so that our relationship with God is no longer estranged. Now, our sins have all been forgiven, and God sees us through the blood of His Son. We can make a new start as stated in 2 Corinthians 5:17:

> *"Therefore If any man be in Christ, he is a new creature: old things are passed away; behold, all things are become new."*

Due to guilt and the pressures of life, many of us do not truly think that our sins have been forgiven. Therefore, as Christians, we need to know who we really are *"in Christ Jesus"*, and that in God's eyes, we are more than "filthy rags".

As Christians, We have a "pick the daisy" (He loves me, He loves me not) view of who God is, and who we are in Him. The Devil has deceived us into thinking that we can never live up to God's standards of holiness and righteousness and that we will always be second best in His eyes. If we are to live out the plan that God has devised for us with complete confidence that we are who *He* says we are, and that we can do all that *He* says we can do, we will need to know our true identity and the inheritance that is ours when we are *"in Christ Jesus."* It is time to come out of the dungeons of our own minds and change our traditionalist thinking patterns about the reality of our relationship with God the Father, Jesus Christ our Savior, and God the Holy Spirit

The purpose of this study is to boost the "spiritual awareness" of those who have accepted Jesus as their Savior and are now members of the "body of Christ".

If you are a new Christian, this study will provide a great starting point for you. As a new believer, there are some truths that you need to know in advance about your present and future walk with Jesus Christ. Knowing and taking a stand on the great truths about who you are now that you are *"In Christ Jesus"* will put you far ahead of the "crowd" as you live your life for Him.

You should know that there are important and necessary things that you as a new Christian already have available to you that will give you a great leap ahead in life as you experience your new found freedom in Christ Jesus. Here are a few of your advantages:

1. First, as the great "Giver", God has given His only Son Jesus as a ransom for your sins. Attached to Jesus' sacrifice is the gift of eternal life. The Bible says in John 3:16-17:

    [16] "For God so loved the world, that he gave his only begotten Son, that whosoever believeth in him should not perish, but have everlasting life. [17] For God sent not his Son into the world

to condemn the world; but that the world through him might be saved".

2. Second, He gave you the Holy Spirit through His Son Jesus Christ. Jesus said: *"And I will pray the Father, and he shall give you another* Comforter, *that he may abide with you forever;"* (John 14:16*)*. Later in the same chapter Jesus makes His commitment to giving to those who are His quite clear when He says:

    "But the Comforter, which is the Holy Ghost, whom the Father will send in my name, he shall teach you all things, and bring all things to your remembrance, whatsoever I have said unto you" John 14:26).

3. Third, He gave you His word that will never fail:

    "The grass withereth, the flower fadeth: but the word of our God shall stand for ever" (Isaiah 40:8*)*. God wants you to learn about Him through reading and then obeying His word. *Jesus said in Matthew 11:28-30:*

    > [28] *"Come unto me, all ye that labour and are heavy laden, and I will give you rest.* [29] *Take my yoke upon you, and learn of me; for I am meek and lowly in heart: and ye shall find rest unto your souls.* [30] *For my yoke is easy, and my burden is light".*

    God also wants you to allow His word to guide you. In the book of Psalms119:105 are these words:

    > *"Thy word is a lamp unto my feet, and a light unto my path".*

4. Fourth, Jesus also gave you spiritual "gifts" that you are to use to edify or build up other Christians: The bible book of Ephesians 4:11-12 explains:

> *[11] And he gave some, apostles; and some, prophets; and some, evangelists; and some, pastors and teachers; [12] For the perfecting of the saints, for the work of the ministry, for the edifying of the body of Christ:"*

These are divine gifts given by God to assist you in your new walk with Christ, and no one can take them away from you: *"For the gifts and calling of God are without repentance" (Romans 11:29).* The New Living Translation of the Bible records the same verse in this manner: *"[29] For God's gifts and his call can never be withdrawn".*

The Bible chronicles the experiences of many faithful heroes, men and women who trusted God's word and prevailed. Hebrews, Chapter 11, often called "The Hall of Faith" gives a list of faithful men and women in Scripture who knew the word of God and lived it, some even unto death. You may already know the stories of saints like Abel, Enoch, Noah, Abraham, Sarah, Isaac, Jacob and Moses, to name a few. Likewise, the Bible also tells of the consequences for many who did not obey God's word and were the worst for it. As new Christians, we are to follow those who have set a *godly* example by showing us how to "live the word". So you see, you already have a great starting advantage. God has already equipped you with gifts that you will need so that you can live the Christian life.

However, there is a word of advice and caution for those in the body of Christ. The Bible warns (through the Apostle Paul) that we are not to allow ourselves to become conceited or arrogant because we are Christians:

> *"For I say, through the grace given unto me, to every man that is among you, not to think of himself more highly than he ought to think; but to think*

soberly, according as God hath dealt to every man the measure of faith" (Romans 12:3).

As Christians, we are to make a conscious, i.e., intentional effort to remain humble. In Matthew 10:16, are these words:

"Behold, I send you forth as sheep in the midst of wolves: be ye therefore wise as serpents, and harmless as doves."

Superior and self-righteous attitudes have no place in God's kingdom. These arrogant attitudes are of "the world", and unless left behind *in* the world, will hinder the work that God has called you to do.

For those who are "seasoned saints" i.e., you have been Christians for a long time, allow this book to boost your spiritual awareness. Look for opportunities to reflect on truths that you know but may have deposited in your memory bank and forgotten. These are the areas that you may need to revisit. Also look for new perspectives you might have missed in earlier bible study. Remember that the Bible has provisions for every situation that you will face; and that there are scriptures that are designed to help you in time of need. The book of 2 Timothy, chapter 3 sums up the reason for God's word by saying:

[16] All scripture is given by inspiration of God, and is profitable for doctrine, for reproof, for correction, for instruction in righteousness: [17] That the man of God may be perfect, thoroughly furnished unto all good works.

You have many God-given gifts. You need to learn how to use them to your advantage with faith, skill, and courage.

Be sure to look for spiritual *"affirmations"* (beginning in chapter 2) throughout this book that are designed to build your confidence as a member of the body of Christ. Blank journal pages are also available at the end of each chapter to assist you in completing each journal assignment.

In Christ Jesus-You are more than filthy rags!

"For ye are all the children of God by faith in Christ Jesus. For as many of you as have been baptized into Christ have put on Christ. There is neither Jew nor Greek, there is neither bond nor free, there is neither male nor female: for ye are all one in Christ Jesus" (Galatians 3:26-28 KJV).

CHAPTER 1

Leaving the Past Behind

When we accepted Jesus as our Savior, we began a new life *"in Christ Jesus."* With that acceptance, our inner man or spirit man was reborn. God gave us the ability to start a new life full of His Spirit. In God's eyes, our old way of living has "passed away", i.e., we are dead to it and to our past sins. Indeed, we are a new "creation" with a new place in God:

> *"For ye are dead, and your life is hid with Christ in God" (Colossians 3:3),* and a new destination:

> *"But now they desire a better country, that is, an heavenly: wherefore God is not ashamed to be called their God: for he hath prepared for them a city" (Hebrews 11:16).*

Yet some would say that even with this new life, God still sees us as "filthy rags". That's because before we were saved, we decided to follow our own way rather than adhere to God's standards of holiness and righteousness. As Christians, we are now more than man's descriptions of human frailties and gross inadequacies. Now that we are saved we are *in Christ Jesus* and adopted into the family of God. We have identified with Him and are indeed sons and daughters of the Most High God. Jesus is now our Savior and our elder brother. Now, God sees us through the blood that Jesus shed on the cross for us.

As humans, it is obvious that our viewpoint of others and ourselves is skewed. The kind of teaching that sees us as never being able to meet God's standards has been programmed into our minds by the "world's" standards. Our thoughts are therefore naturally cloudy-making our opinions of each other like looking through muddy waters, i.e., extremely "murky" at best. When the "world" looks at us and at others, it automatically sees the worst. When God looks at us, He already knows the best about us because He knows what He has destined us to become. He's the One who gave us our destiny. He also knows the beginning and end of us. The prophet Jeremiah spoke of God's thoughts for us in Jeremiah 29:11:

> *"For I know the plans and thoughts that I have for you"*, *says the LORD, plans for peace and well -being and not for disaster to give you a future and a hope"* (The Amplified Bible).

God indeed sees us from a different perspective. To Him we are of much more value than what *others inside and outside of the body of Christ* may say or think. God does not see us from man's carnal viewpoint:

> *"But the LORD said unto Samuel, Look not on his countenance, or on the height of his stature; because I have refused him: for the LORD seeth not as man seeth; for man looketh on the outward appearance, but the LORD looketh on the heart" (1 Samuel 16:7).*

Since we belong to God, He does not see us with eyes of condemnation. He sees us with eyes of love, for He is love (1 John 4:8) and has always known our marvelous potential. Would God have said *"Be ye holy for I am holy* (Leviticus 19:2; 1 Peter 1:15) if He did not think that we could meet that standard? We must always remember that it is only what *God* thinks of us that will make *any* difference in this life and in the life to come.

Believing in and accepting Jesus as our Savior gave us eternal (a life in God's presence that lasts forever) life (John 3:16). In John 5:24, Jesus said:

> *"Verily, verily, I say unto you, he that heareth my word, and believeth on Him that sent me, hath everlasting life and shall not come into condemnation; but is passed from death unto life".*

Hallelujah! Our old "self" has passed away. Our slate, as it were, has been wiped clean by the blood of Jesus. Another more poignant Scripture brings our status in Christ into crystal clear focus:

> *"There is therefore now no condemnation to them which are in Christ Jesus, who walk not after the flesh but after the Spirit. For the law of the Spirit of life in Christ Jesus hath made me free from the law of sin and death" (Romans 8:1-2).*

Glory to God! There is new blood coursing through our veins! Our spirit man has been reborn. We are free! For this, we should be continually rejoicing. Yet, we have not learned to leave the past behind. In many instances we still find ourselves wallowing in guilt and poor self-image because of who others who knew us before our "metamorphosis"–our great change- say that we are, and because of this love/hate relationship we have with ourselves. We must begin to release ourselves from the guilt that we felt when we were unsaved. That was then, this is now. God has removed our sins far from us, so why should we continue to dredge them up out of the mire, lift them high for all to see, and say to the world, "See, this is what I did. This is what I once was." Each time we do this, evil spirits of condemnation and guilt come in to influence our thinking. We have opened the door for the enemy to attack everything that we have, including our character and testimony. The Devil will step in and attempt to further cloud our minds and destroy our relationship with Christ as he says: "See, I told you you'd never measure up to *His* standards. He requires too much of you. You'll never change. You are what you've always been, so you might as well give up and accept who you are." Instead of stopping our ears to this mental harassment and immoral "mumbo jumbo", we listen and allow our minds to become saturated with his words of discouragement and condemnation; while at the same time, completely ignoring the truth that the word of God says about us.

Satan (the Devil) is aware that as long as we believe that we are still what we used to be, we will never attempt to fully walk in the freedom and holy calling that God has planned for us. His desire is that we will be limp, lethargic Christians; and that we will continue to think that we can't or won't be able to live up to the standards of holiness and love to which God has called us. In addition, our feelings of guilt and unworthiness will make us hesitant and fearful to answer and be obedient to God's calling for our lives.

As Christians, we seem to have a problem realizing that God has forgiven us and that our past sins have been removed. We simply want to hold on as tightly as we can to our old feelings of guilt. After all, guilt has been our constant companion for many years. We have come to feel comfortable with it. It is as if we have cleaned ourselves up, then gone right back and put on the dirty, stinking clothes that we wore before we were washed clean.

A good example of this appears in the biblical rendition of the "prodigal son" as found in Luke, chapter 15:11-24. The younger son asked his father for his inheritance even when he knew that it was not due him at the time. He ignored his father's wishes, the traditions of his people, and overlooked his elder brother to get what he thought was his. He did not care that when he asked for his inheritance, it affected his brother's also. No, his request for his inheritance did not "break his father's bank" because at the end of the account, the father was still a rich man with servants and land.

After his father granted his request, he went far away from home (where he thought no one would know or see how he lived) and wasted his father's inheritance with "riotous living". He had no plans for the future, just "eat, drink and be merry." When the inheritance was gone and his so-called friends had abandoned him, he found himself desirous of eating slop with the pigs he had been hired to feed. Imagine the putrid smell of a pigpen; then imagine the horror he felt while feeding swine, the very animals that were repulsive to his people. Imagine his emaciated body-skin and bones- indicating that he had hit rock bottom. That could cause anyone to think about going home.

His current situation made him begin to consider what he had done. *"When he came to himself"* by realizing what a wasteful, sinful, disobedient, hurtful life he had been living, he remembered the loving father he had left behind. This son then made the best decision of his life:

> *"And when he came to himself, he said, "How many hired servants of my father's have bread enough and to spare, and I perish with hunger! I will arise and go to my father and will say unto him, Father, I have sinned against heaven, and before thee, and am no more worthy to be called thy son: make me as one of thy hired servants" (Luke 15:17-19).*

He would have been satisfied to have his lot cast with the servants in his father's household. At least they were fed properly, and were under their master's care and protection.

When he arrived home, he had no thoughts of his former station in life. In fact, he did not expect much from his father. But he received much more than he had ever dreamed:

"And he arose and came to his father. But when he was yet a great way off, his father saw him, and had compassion, and ran, and fell on his neck, and kissed him… the father said to his servants, Bring forth the best robe, and put it on him; and put a ring on his hand, and shoes on his feet; and bring hither the fatted calf, and kill it; and let us eat, and be merry: For this my son was dead, and is alive again; he was lost, and is found. And they began to be merry" (Luke 15:20, 22-24).

Notice that the father did not run to the son and bring up all of his past deeds. Nor did he slap his face and call him dirty names because of what he had done. Sure, he had heard the awful reports about his son's conduct. The older brother attests to this in his anger by reminding the father that this wayward son had *"devoured thy living [livelihood] with harlots" (Luke 15:30).* Yet, in the midst of it all, the father ran to welcome his son home. You can be sure that not a day went by without this father thinking on his lost son. In spite of his son's sins, the father recognized his value to the family and the kingdom and received him with joy.

Once we were in the "pig pen" eating with nasty, filthy, stinking swine of the world. We did anything that we were big enough and bad enough to do. We knew that what we were doing was wrong but were powerless to break free on our own. We were "stuck in the mire" as it were. Then, "when we came to ourselves" through circumstances and experiences that made us realize our miserable state, we made a conscious decision to leave the slop of life, and return home. We did this by accepting the salvation that had already been made available to us. We came back to our Father God, through His Son Jesus Christ.

Just as the father welcomed the son back into the fold, God welcomes us when we are truly repentant. He receives us with joy, love and compassion:

"I say unto you, that likewise joy shall be in heaven over one sinner that repenteth, more than over ninety and nine just persons, which need no repentance" *(Luke 15:7).*

For some of us, it is hard to break old habits. We persist in our condemnation of ourselves. What we fail to realize is that God does not condemn those who are *in Christ Jesus.* We condemn ourselves and allow Satan to do the same. Jesus' blood has cleansed us and God has removed the old sins from us. The Scriptures say: *"As far as the east is from the west, so far hath he removed our transgressions from us" (Psalm 103:12).* When we made the decision to accept Jesus, God put our past sins in a place where they would neither meet us again nor be remembered by Him. Despite the great distance that has been placed between us and our sins, we continue to remind God, the "world, and ourselves about who or what we once were. We do not realize that we are assisting the enemy to tear down our spiritual character and weaken our testimony.

Whether you know it or not, there is a war going on in the spirit world. Just as the Devil continually fights against God, your flesh continuously fights against the Spirit of God in you (See Romans 7:18-21). Satan wants to keep us in a state of uncertainty regarding our newly found relationship with Christ. His aim is to weaken us by using doubt and guilt to kill the strength that is growing within us while we are yet saplings. He wants to destroy our Christian influence in this world before it has a chance to take root, become supernaturally charged, and spread like wildfire.

When we listen with our minds to Satan's constant words of attack and condemnation through others and ourselves, his spirit of negativism and disapproval is intertwined with our spirits. In effect, then, we are aiding and abetting the enemy, and we know that he is always looking for a way to *"steal, kill, and destroy" (John 10:10).* We are in essence "sleeping with the enemy" who is definitely wide-awake and watching for any advantage or "weak link" that he can find in us. He would like nothing more than to keep us weak-minded by keeping our past before us so that we will not have the gumption to act, even on our own behalf. Satan wants to keep us bound. He does not want us to realize that we have the supernatural, God-given power and authority to break free, and stay free.

We must then remember that one of the greatest truths that we have going for us is that Jesus Christ died to bring us back into fellowship with God the Father. Now we belong to Him; and because we are His, no one, especially the Devil, can snatch us out of His hand (John 10:28). Neither can anyone or anything change God's mind about us.

We can rest assured that God alone knows our frame and our hearts. He knew us before we knew ourselves (Psalm 71:6). He knows all about us including who we once were, who we are now, and who we will become. We are the ones who catch on to the "buzz-words" of the past, and since they still *sound* good, convince ourselves that they are truth. Thus, we continue to perpetuate those archaic, teetering on the edge of blasphemous "mind-sets" from generation to generation.

God tells us that we are a *"new creature"* (2 Corinthians 5:17). We respond by saying, "No God. I wish that that were true, but remember when I used to stand on the corner selling drugs? Remember when I committed adultery? Do you remember when I stole from my neighbor?" In many instances, we are the ones who keep telling God that we are worthless.

It seems that the hardest thing for us to accept is that we truly have been forgiven, and that we have been changed. This could be because God, being the loving and kind Father that He is, did not take a hammer, hit us over the head with it and say: "There, that did it! Now feel the pain and the lump on your head so that you can be sure that you have been changed." God wants us to *"walk by faith and not by sight"* (2 Corinthians 5:7) fully believing that a sinner's cry to a loving Father can catapult us into eternal life.

We must begin to consider that despite what we think about ourselves, God has and knows the best plan for our lives. Again, the prophet Jeremiah said:

"For I know the thoughts that I think toward you, saith the Lord; thoughts of peace and not of evil, to give you and expected end [a future and a hope]" (Jeremiah 29:11).

God's thoughts are not our thoughts, and His ways are certainly not our ways (Isaiah 55:8). God is not like man. Man is inclined to forgive, but never forget (in the sense that man will remember your former faults especially when you have offended him again). Some will continually remember your old faults and may even try to "dig" up those that you've long buried. God is not like man who when offended will find some way of getting even. He does not forgive us, then turn around and throw our sins back into our faces to see how guilty He can make us feel. That what the enemy does. God is not that kind of God. He is holy, loving and quite different from anything that we can imagine. He wants us to live a victorious life, being thankful that we have been changed and grateful to Him as we realize *"Whose"* we are. God wants us to walk in confidence, knowing that whatever "good work" He has begun in us will be accomplished. The apostle Paul put forth this thought when he said:

"Being confident of this very thing, that he which hath begun a good work in you will perform [complete] it until the day of Jesus Christ" (Philippians 1:6).

We have a "promised land" available to us wherein God has mapped out His perfect will for our lives. However, we will be hard pressed to triumph over Satan, our adversary, stay in the battle, and possess our land if we see ourselves merely as insignificant "grasshoppers". That is how the Devil wants us to think so that he can squash us like the insects *we* think we are, and accomplish his plan against us. We aid the enemy when we allow ourselves to "think" as he wants us to think. It is therefore imperative that we change our thinking patterns. We must believe that we are truly *"accepted of the Beloved" (Ephesians 1:6)* and are therefore of great value to

God, and that He wants us to know it! In 1 Corinthians 1:30, we find these words:

> *"But of Him are ye in Christ Jesus, who of God is made unto us wisdom, and righteousness, and sanctification, and redemption."*

I am in Christ Jesus. I choose to believe God. What about you? Whose report about you or anything else will you believe?

CHAPTER 2

Testifying... "Telling It Like It Is" You Have a Testimony

"Mortify therefore your members which are upon the earth; fornication, uncleanness, inordinate affection [passion], evil concupiscence [desire] and covetousness, which is idolatry, for which things sakes the wrath [extreme anger, vengeance] of God cometh on the children of disobedience; In the which ye also walked some time, when ye lived in them" (Colossians 3:5-7, explanation in brackets mine).

In several passages in the Bible, (1 Corinthians 6:11; Colossians 3:5-7) the apostle Paul spoke of the former state of those in the "body of Christ" who were once non-believers. He spoke not to bring shame to them, nor to remind them from whence they came, nor to open old wounds that had long since healed; but to show where they stood in relation to Christ Jesus *now*. Paul also wanted to exhort Christians to continue in this new and living Way.

Sometimes those in the churches that were established by Paul had to be dealt with regarding patterns of thinking that brought on attitudes deviating from the truth. These shifts in thinking had been erroneously introduced into the church by some well-intentioned and some not so well-intentioned teachers and leaders. Paul knew that if these thought patterns were allowed to continue, there would be divisions and ultimately, heresy in the church. The apostle Paul did not "bite his tongue" during the times that he had to chastise Christian believers. He told them exactly the way things were and the way things should be.

In 1 Corinthians, chapter 6, Paul rebuked those in the Corinthian church about their habit of taking each other to court to settle matters before unjust judges:

> "Dare any of you, having a matter against another, go to law before the unjust and not before the saints? ...I speak to your shame [Shame on you!]. Is it so that there is not a wise man among you? No, not one that shall be able to judge between his brethren? Now therefore there is utterly a fault among you, because ye go to law one with another. Why do you not rather take wrong? Why do you not rather suffer yourself to be defrauded? Nay, you do wrong and defraud, and that your brethren. Know ye not that the unrighteous shall not inherit the kingdom of God? Be not deceived: neither fornicators, nor idolaters, nor adulterers, nor effeminate, nor abusers of themselves with mankind, nor thieves, nor covetous, nor drunkards, nor revilers, nor extortioners, shall inherit the kingdom of God. AND SUCH WERE SOME OF YOU: BUT (emphasis mine) ye are washed, but ye are sanctified, but ye are justified in the name of the Lord Jesus, and by the Spirit of our God" (1 Corinthians 6:1; 5-11; brackets and emphasis mine).

Paul gave a "dirty laundry list" of unrighteous deeds that had permeated the saints *before* they were saved. Now here they were taking their brethren to court in front of the same kind of folk that they had once been. After his firm chastisement, Paul tells the saints that they must remember that they are not the same anymore. They indeed have been transformed, cleansed, sanctified (set apart), and made right by the blood of Jesus. Paul was saying, "Let me remind you of the things that God will not tolerate. *Remember also that these are the very things that you once did.* You are not like that anymore, so why are you acting in your former manner? You have been changed." Paul was not chiding them because of who they once were, but was letting them know that they must remember that they were now *"better than that."* Paul had no qualms about "telling it like it was."

Another aspect that is most noteworthy in Paul's life was his remarkable habit of testifying about the power of the living God- because of his life-changing encounter with Jesus on the road to Damascus (see Acts, chapter 9). Paul knew that he had had an experience that he would never forget. He also knew that he could not keep the story to himself. He had to tell somebody. Thus, at every opportunity, Paul told of his conversion on the road to Damascus. He spoke to any who would listen, even to kings, governors and potentates. Whether they were "almost persuaded" (Acts 26:28) or fully persuaded, Paul humbly, yet with much skill, told his story.

Paul's testifying was much different from the habit we have today, of beating ourselves up at every opportunity by reopening wounds that Jesus has already healed. His testifying was much different from the old church tradition where some members arose to tell all of their "business" because they had a captive audience. More importantly, Paul knew that all that he said and all that he did was to be done so that the glory would go to God and God alone. Paul's testimony spoke to the fact that "it's not about me": *It is no longer "I", but Christ living in me" (Galatians 2:20).* Paul's testimony was therefore more of "See where the Lord has brought me from, and look at what He has done for me!"

When Paul told his story, he told it truthfully-with conviction and sincerity. He also told it so that others could be persuaded to come to know and love a kind and forgiving God as he did, (If

God can forgive me, I know He will forgive you). He knew that the church was to be edified by his words. He also knew that Christians were charged to edify, i.e., build up each other. What better way for Paul to build up others than by giving glory to God for bringing him out of the "mess" that he was in. Paul thus set an example for Christians through the ages to follow. He told his story because he was certain that there was someone who could benefit from it. There was someone going through something that needed to know that they were not alone. There was someone who would hear a word from him and want to follow his example. Paul knew that there was someone who would hear his testimony and decide to follow Jesus.

Another who was not at all hesitant to tell her story was the Samaritan woman in John, chapter 4. She was the woman at the well who after meeting and communing with Jesus, left her water pots and ran to town exclaiming: *"Come, see a man, which told me all things that ever I did: is not this the Christ?" (John 4:29).*

Like the Samaritan woman, and like Paul, we need to tell our story. In fact, we need to come out of our comfort zones, "leave our water pots" and go tell all that we have an opportunity to tell about just how good God has been to us. We do not have to dredge up the past by digging deep into our storehouse of long healed and forgiven hurts. If we think that we need to tell things in our past that will help someone else, we should tell our story in such a way that all the glory goes to God because of how He brought us through and out of it. We belong to God. We are not ashamed of Him or His gospel, and we want the world to know it!

Affirmation #1: We belong to the Lord!"

"For whether we live, we live unto the Lord; and whether we die, we die unto the Lord: whether we live therefore, or die, we are the Lord's." Romans 14:8

Your Assignment:

- Think about your life and the changes that have come about since you had your conversion experience. Then, tell your story. How did you meet Jesus? How has knowing Him changed your life? Are there any Scriptures that would fit into your story?
- Begin looking at who you are in Christ Jesus by writing your own personal testimony in your journal. Remember to make you story of salvation one that will glorify God the Father.
- Finished? Now, go tell it. Ask God to lead you to an opportunity to witness by sharing your story with someone who is not saved.
- What were the results of this encounter? Record those experiences in your journal too.

Journal   Date_____

CHAPTER 3

Now We Are "In Christ"

"Therefore if any man be in Christ, he is a new creature [creation]; old things are passed away; behold all things are become new" (2 Corinthians 5:17).

Think for a moment of a certified letter that arrives at your home address. Without opening it, you already know that there is an important message inside for someone. That's because your signature is required in order to accept it. As you examine your letter, you find that even if you do not open it, there is value in its contents. The mere fact that you have had to sign for it proclaims its value to the person who sent it since they thought the contents were important enough to insure.

A continued careful examination indicates that you can write on the outside of the envelope. You can spill food, or drink or any other liquid on the outside and have no effect on the contents inside. Whatever is inside is protected. The contents are still neatly folded and clean. In addition, the message inside has not been changed at all. It continues to have the same meaning. It still has a purpose and value. That's a very simple analogy of those of us who are in

Christ Jesus. We are certified, i.e., signed, sealed, and delivered by the power of the blood of Jesus Christ. We have a message of hope, deliverance and life for those inside and outside of the body of Christ. We are enveloped, and protected by the blood of Jesus-our holy covering.

We are indeed "in Christ Jesus" because we have accepted his gracious and free offer of salvation and are now a part of His glorious body. We now belong to God and identify with Him. Yet, there is so much more to our being "in Christ Jesus." In his book, *The Christian Disciple's Manual (1992),* David Kirkwood explains more of what being *"in Christ"* means. He says:

"Throughout the New Testament, we find numerous phrases such as *in Christ, with Christ,* and *in Him.* Most often these phrases refer to some benefit that we, as believers, possess because of what Jesus has done for us. If we are ever going to see ourselves as God Himself sees us, we must first see ourselves "in Christ." What does it mean to be "in Christ"? Simply this: Now that we have been born again, we have been placed into Christ's body and are vitally joined with him:

> *"...So we who are many, are one body in Christ" (Romans 12:5a).*

> *But by His doing, you are in Christ Jesus, who became to us wisdom from God, and righteousness and sanctification, and redemption..." Now we are Christ's body, and individually members of it" (1 Corinthians 1:30; 12:27)[1].*

> The above scripture reveals several blessings that are ours by virtue of being "in Christ". We have been redeemed (purchased from slavery), sanctified (set apart by and for God) and made right (given right-standing with God)! Hallelujah!"[1]

When we were born again by accepting Jesus as our Lord and Savior, we became new creatures. We were changed. As a result of that change, we now identify with Jesus Christ and have turned away (repented or made a deliberate change) from the attitudes and sinful acts we did before we knew Him. Being a new creature, however, does not mean that the problems and daily cares of this world cannot and will not spill over on us. Jesus lived a sin-free life (2 Corinthians 5:21), but He did not have an "issue-free" life while here on earth. Neither can we escape earthly perils, trials and persecutions. The apostle Paul made this plain to believers when he said: *"Yea, and all that will live godly in Christ Jesus shall suffer persecution" (2 Timothy 3:12).* In fact, because of the newness of life in Christ, more issues (many brought on by demon forces; some brought on by our immaturity in Christ) and challenges than usual may arise.

Now that you are "in Christ" you have identified with Him. You must be aware that walking in your newly found relationship will definitely bring on an all-out assault by your adversary, the Devil. He is God's enemy and yours, too. The Devil hates God, and His Son Jesus. He also hates everything that is connected with them. You have been removed from his evil grasp. Expect him to come after you seeking to *regain* (John 10:10) that which he has lost. He will do this by tempting you to sin, and by attempting to rob you of your faith and your testimony. You are therefore to be watchful and mindful of his attacks. More importantly, you are to study God's word so that you will become sober and vigilant, be prepared for his attacks, and use God's word as a weapon. As the apostle Peter admonished, you are to:

> *"Be sober, be vigilant; because your adversary the devil, as a roaring lion, walketh about, seeking whom he may devour" (1 Peter 5:8).*

The apostle Paul also knew that even though temptations, persecutions and trials will come, there is always victory in Christ Jesus. He thus gave these words of encouragement:

"There hath no temptation taken you but such as is common to man, but God is faithful, who will not suffer you to be tempted above that ye are able, but will with the temptation also make a way to escape, that ye may be able to bear it" (1 Corinthians 10:13).

As Christians we must know that "in Christ Jesus, we are able to bear extraordinary challenges while waiting on our deliverance. We must know that God is faithful to perform His word, and has already made a way for us to escape.

It is true that Satan will attempt to snatch us out of God's ark of safety. There will even be times when we may not see a way out of our temptations and trials with our natural eyes. But be assured that we need not "see" a thing to believe that it is there. We just need to keep our focus and *"...run with patience the race that is set before us, looking unto Jesus the author and finisher of our faith;" (Hebrews 12:1, 2).* Yes, He has finished our faith, and thank God, He already knows what the end is going to be.

We also need to look to the wisdom that God has given us in His word. The Scriptures say:

"God is not a man, that He should lie; neither the son of man, that He should repent: hath He said, and shall He not do it? Or hath He spoken, and shall He not make it good?" (Numbers23:19).

This positive affirmation must also seep deep down into our spirits: God will "make it good": *"And we know that all things work together for good to them that love God, to them who are the called according to his purpose" (Romans 8:28).*

Even when others seek to "steam away" our faith by opening us up to the world, i.e., reminding the world of what we used to be before we cast our identity with Christ, we are sealed in Christ Jesus through His blood and the power of the Holy Spirit. It does not matter what *they* say, because God will place a hedge of protection around us that will keep us "enveloped" in a place of safety and security. This we must catch hold of and believe no matter what comes our way. We can then maintain our spiritual strength as we keep our "spiritual" eyes focused on the one true God who sustains us all.

Finally, when we are in Christ Jesus, we belong to Him. Our position as children of the living God rises to new heights. In fact, our faith increases more and more as we learn God's word and put it into practice by obeying and putting our trust in Him. For it is then that we realize that it is has always been *"In Him that we live and move and have our being," (Acts 17:28);* and that we can do nothing without Him (John 15:5). Thus, when the world attempts to isolate us so that we feel that we are alone, away from God, Jesus becomes our "All", our "Everything," our Rock, our Shield, and our Buckler. He is our hiding place, our Deliverer and *"a very present help in time of trouble" (Psalm 46:1b).*

When we are in Christ Jesus, we are anchored in a sure and firm foundation. We are also in a position where we can benefit others, i.e., our *neighbors* whoever they are. We can safely and confidently fulfill our mission to *"go ye into all the world and preach the gospel to every creature" (Mark 16:15).* God is faithful. He is "real", and will do what He says He will do. Just believe Him.

Affirmation #2: "Your faith in Christ Jesus and acceptance of Him as your Savior makes you a child of God, and the seed of Abraham."

> *"...For ye are all the children of God by faith in Christ Jesus. For as many of you as have been baptized into Christ have put on Christ. There is neither Jew nor Greek, there is neither bond nor free, there is neither male nor female: for ye are all one in Christ Jesus. And if ye [be] Christ's, then are ye Abraham's seed, and heirs according to the promise." Galatians 3:26-29*

Here is your next assignment:

> **Your Assignment:** Think about your daily experiences relating to how the Lord has protected you and kept you even when you were going through trials, tribulations, persecutions and temptations. In your journal, write your thoughts relating what it meant to you during these times to be *"in Christ Jesus."*
>
> Remember to thank and praise God for all that He has done for you. Thank Him for the "seen" (those things that you saw with your own eyes and know that He prevented from happening in your life) and the "unseen" (those things that happened to you that when you look back you did not "see" coming but you know that "if it had not been for the Lord on your side" (Psalm 124:1-2) you would not have made it through. Without His divine intervention, you would not have escaped from a traffic accident, survived the death of a loved one, been healed from sickness and/ or disease, been delivered from financial troubles, conquered emotional issues, etc. You are protected and enveloped in Christ Jesus. Continue to tell your story.

Journal   Date_____

CHAPTER 4

"Heirs and Joint-heirs" In Christ Jesus

"For if we live after the flesh, ye shall die: but if ye through the Spirit do mortify the deeds of the body, ye shall live. For as many as are led by the Spirit of God, they are the sons of God. For ye have not received the spirit of bondage again to fear; but ye have received the Spirit of adoption; whereby we cry, Abba, Father. The Spirit itself beareth witness with our spirit, that we are the children of God: And if children, then heirs; heirs of God, and joint-heirs with Christ; if so be that we suffer with him, that we may also be glorified together" (Romans 8:13-17).

According to *Merriam Webster's Online Dictionary (2009)* an heir is defined in several ways:

1. *"one who inherits or is entitled to inherit property;*
2. *one who inherits or is entitled to succeed to a hereditary rank, title, or office;*
3. *one who receives or is entitled to receive some endowment or quality from a parent or predecessor."*[2]

Just as there are different kinds of inheritances, there are different ways to be in line for an inheritance. One way is to obtain a portion or all of an owner's goods or property after his death. Another is to be assigned a portion or lot by God. One can even inherit while the benefactor is still alive, as evidenced by the biblical account of the "Prodigal Son" (Luke 15).

During Bible times, a father's property was divided among the sons of his legitimate wives, with the eldest son getting the larger portion. Here is an example using a truth about land inheritance as explained in *Eaton's Bible Dictionary (1992):* "keeping land in the tribe began with keeping it in the family."[3].

In the book of Numbers God gave Moses the basic laws of family inheritance:

> *"If a man dies, and has no son, then you shall cause his inheritance to pass to his daughter. And if he has no daughter, then you shall give his inheritance to his brothers. And if he has no brothers, then you shall give his inheritance to his father's brothers. And if his father has no brothers, then you shall give his inheritance to his kinsman that is next to him of his family..." (Numbers 27:8-11).*

Notice also that daughters were included in the line of family inheritance.

The Bible says that when we become Christians, we become "heirs and joint-heirs with Jesus Christ": *"And if children, then heirs; heirs of God, and joint-**heirs** with Christ;" (Romans 8:17a).* A joint-heir is one who receives a portion of an estate, rank, title, or office. In the natural, it seems unthinkable that God has made us partakers in His Son's inheritance.

Now that we belong to Christ, God is our Father, and Jesus is our elder brother. This is true because the acceptance of Jesus as our Savior ushered in our adoption as one of His Father's children. We are now related to Jesus and thus also sons and daughters of the Most

High God. Therefore, we share in what Jesus receives. Be assured that God has more than enough to spread around. *Everything* already belongs to Him: *"The earth is the Lord's and the fullness thereof; the world, and they that dwell within" (Psalm 24:1).*

The apostle Paul was one who understood the "mystery of Christ" as relates to Gentile heir-ship and made it clear to the believers at Ephesus when he said:

> *"Surely you have heard about the administration of God's grace that was given to me for you, that is, the mystery made known to me by revelation, as I have already written briefly. In reading this, then, you will be able to understand my insight into the mystery of Christ, which was not made known to men in other generations as it has now been revealed by the Spirit to God's holy apostles and prophets. THIS MYSTERY IS THAT THROUGH THE GOSPEL THE GENTILES ARE HEIRS TOGETHER WITH ISRAEL, MEMBERS TOGETHER OF ONE BODY, AND SHARERS TOGETHER IN THE PROMISE IN CHRIST JESUS" (Ephesians 3:2-6, capitalization mine).*

Paul said that the fact that we as Gentile Christians will be fellow-heirs with Christ through means of the gospel was a truth that had been hidden from the patriarchs of old, but revealed to him and the apostles and prophets by the Holy Spirit. Again, Paul put it plainly in Galatians 3:29: *"And if ye be Christ's, then are ye Abraham's seed, and heirs according to the promise."* Here is God's promise to Abraham as found in Genesis 12:3:

> *"And I will bless them that bless thee, and curse him that curseth thee: and in thee shall all families of the earth be blessed."*

The "mystery" has been solved. We can see that from the very beginning, it was God's plan to include us as heirs along with His Son Jesus Christ. It was never His intention to leave us out of His holy plan. How wonderful that this exciting mystery is also revealed to saints of today through the Holy Scriptures!

It is awesome to think that God loves us so much that He is willing to allow us to share in the inheritance with Jesus. After all, we are not the ones who died on the cross; and we know that we deserved to pay with our lives for our own sins. Think how blessed we are to have a Savior who paid the ultimate price for us, and yet has no qualms about sharing His "portion" with us.

What then is Jesus' inheritance or portion? In order to be specific about the things that Jesus has inherited, we need to know what things belong to God the Father. According to the following Scripture, everything belongs to God:

> "Thine, O Lord, is the greatness, and the power, and the glory, and the victory and the majesty: for all that is in the heaven and the earth is thine; thine is the kingdom, O Lord, and thou art exalted as the head above all. Both riches and honour come of thee, and thou reignest over all; and in thine hand is power and might; and in thine hand it is to make great, and to give strength unto all. Now therefore, our God, we thank thee, and praise thy glorious name" (1 Chronicles 29:11-13).

Here are some other scriptures that make God's ownership of all things quite plain:

- **_World/Earth_**- "For every beast is mine, and the cattle upon a thousand hills... for the world is mine and the fullness thereof" (Psalm 50:10, 12).
  "...For all the earth is mine" (Exodus 19:5d).

- **_Souls-_** *"Behold all souls are mine; as the soul of the father, so also the soul of the son is mine: the soul that sinneth, it shall die" (Ezekiel 18:4).*
- **_Wealth-_** *"The silver is mine, and the gold is mine, saith the Lord of hosts" (Haggai 2:8).*
- **_Power-_** *"God hath spoken once, twice have I heard this; that power belongeth unto God" (Psalm 62:11).*
- **_Mercy-_** *"Also unto thee O Lord, belongeth mercy; for thou renderest to every man according to his work" (Psalm 62:12).*
- **_Vengeance-_** *"O Lord God, to whom vengeance belongeth; O God, to who vengeance belongeth, shew thyself" (Psalm 94:1; see also Hebrews 10:30, Deut. 32:35).*
- **_Righteousness-_** *"O Lord, righteousness belongeth unto thee..." (Daniel 9:7a).*
- **_The Sabbath-_** *"But the seventh day is the Sabbath of the Lord thy God..." (Exodus 20:10).*
- **_The Tithe-_** *"And all the tithe of the land, whether of the seed of the land, or of the fruit of the tree, is the Lord's; it is holy unto the Lord" (Leviticus 27:30; Malachi 3:10).*
- **_A Host of Angels-_** *"And Jacob went on his way, and the angels of God met him. And when Jacob saw them, he said, This is God's host; and he called the name of that place Mahanaim" (Genesis 32:1-2).*

From this sampling of the Scriptures, we can see that God has more than enough to meet our every need. Everything tangible and intangible already belongs to Him!

Jesus also gave a true picture of the things that He inherited from God when he said:

> *"All things are delivered to me of my Father: and no man knoweth who the Son is, but the Father; and who the Father is, but the Son, and he to whom the Son will reveal him" (Luke 10:22).*

Since Jesus was given all things, as heirs and joint-heirs with Him, we can share in them also. There are even some things that we are compelled and obligated to give back to God (our souls, the tithe, our praise, our worship).

It is hard for some of us to think that all that we have belongs to God. After all, our natural minds tell us that we are the ones who worked hard for many years to get what we wanted. Our mind whispers that we are the ones who struggled to get an education and make a life for ourselves. We are the ones who pulled ourselves up by our own bootstraps. We indeed are self-made men and women. *Or so we think.* The Psalmist refutes our attitude and says:

> *"I will lift up mine eyes unto the hills, from whence cometh my help. My help cometh from the Lord, which made heaven and earth" (Psalm 121:1-2).*

Even David the king of Israel realized that he could do nothing apart from God:

> *"If it had not been for the Lord on our side when men rose up against us: Then they had swallowed us up quick, when their wrath was kindled against us" (Psalm 124:1, 2).*

As Christians, we need to stop looking at the "stuff" we think we own as the measure of our success in life. Do we not realize that God watched over us and prevented many things seen and unseen from thwarting His plans for our success? It was God who gave us everything we have (our earthly and spiritual inheritance) and prevented the enemy from coming in to steal and annihilate us.

The best thing that we can do then is to commit what God has given us back to Him for safekeeping. Often, we do not realize that when we commit everything that we own back into God's care, He blesses it and multiplies it because our actions demonstrate our willingness to put our complete trust and confidence in Him to *"supply all of our needs according to His riches in glory by Christ Jesus" (Philippians 4:19).* It tells Him that we are willing to stop grabbing for all that we can get, and put the interests of others above our own. Giving what we have back to God takes our focus away from the "stuff" that we own, and leaves room to keep our eyes fastened on Him and His will for our lives. We will then not be burdened with the care of our inheritance anymore. We can be sure that when we sow everything that we own back into God's hands, He will take care of it and multiply it even more so that it produces much fruit for the kingdom.

Once we as Christians recognize that God is the source of all things, our arrogant, "big-headed" attitude (which is not Christ-like) will be replaced with that of a grateful heart. We would also realize the vast blessings that God has made available to us. Even more than that, we would recognize the enormity of His love for us. For as joint-heirs with Jesus Christ, there is a storehouse of wealth (spiritual and physical) owned by God the Father and His Son Jesus, which is accessible to those of us who are "in Christ Jesus"; and it is available for the asking.

We should not be hesitant in approaching or asking because God takes delight in giving to us the things that are His. The gospel of Luke says:

> *"Fear not, little flock; for it is your Father's good pleasure to give to you the kingdom" (Luke 12:32).*

David grabbed hold of this truth when he said:

> *"Let them shout for joy, and be glad that favor my righteous cause: yea, let them say continually, Let the Lord be magnified, which hath pleasure in the prosperity of his servants" (Psalm 35:27).*

God enjoys giving, especially to those in the body of Christ. He takes pleasure in seeing His children prosper. When we are disobedient, He chastises and disciplines (Hebrews 12:6) us because He loves us and wants to bring us back in line with His good plans for our lives.

One last Scripture neatly explains our heir-ship:

> *"And because ye are sons, God hath sent forth the Spirit of his Son into your hearts crying Abba Father: "Wherefore thou art no longer a servant, but a son; and if a son, then an heir of God through Christ" (Galatians 4:6-7).*

Even in the midst of all or our shortcomings, God still wants us to be heirs and joint-heirs, sharing in all of the inheritance of His Son Jesus.

The apostle Peter spoke of our inheritance when he said:

> *"Blessed be the God and Father of our Lord Jesus Christ, which according to his abundant mercy hath begotten us again unto a lively hope by the resurrection of Jesus Christ from the dead, 4 To an inheritance incorruptible, and undefiled, and that fadeth not away, reserved in heaven for you, 5 Who are kept by the power of God through faith unto salvation ready to be revealed in the last time" (1 Peter 1:3-5).*

The great news about our inheritance is not only do we have an inheritance of "things" on the earth, but we also have an *incorruptible* inheritance in heaven. You will not get it all here. You have a far greater inheritance waiting for you in heaven.

In his best-selling book, *The Purpose Driven Life (2002),* author Rick Warren also tells us that we will inherit even more than we realize. Warren says:

> *"What exactly does that inheritance include? First, we will get to be with God forever [see 1 Thessalonians*

4:17; 5:10]. <u>Second</u>, we will be completely changed to be like Christ [see 1 John 3:2; 2 Corinthians 3:18]. <u>Third</u>, we will be freed from all pain, death, and suffering [see Revelations 21:4]. <u>Fourth</u>, we will be rewarded and reassigned positions of service [see Mark 9:41; Mark 10:30; 1 Corinthians 3:8; Hebrews 10:35; and Matthew 25:21-23]; <u>Fifth</u>, we will get to share in Christ's glory [see Romans 8:17; Colossians 3:4; 2 Thessalonians 2:14; 2 Timothy 2:12; 1 Peter 5:1]."[14] (Portions underlined for emphasis).

God's inheritance is not only applicable to this world, but reaches out into the distance across time-into the world to come, into eternity. Jesus has gone so far as to prepare a place for us so that we can forever be with Him and the Father. This means that we can let go of the "things of this world", for when we are "in Christ Jesus" we quickly come to the realization that this world is not our home. This life is indeed temporary. We are citizens of heaven. Jesus made this clear as He spoke to His disciples:

> *"Let not your heart be troubled: ye believe in God, believe also in me. In my Father's house are many mansions: if it were not so, I would have told you: I go to prepare a place for you. And if I go and prepare a place for you; I will come again and receive you unto myself; that where I am, there ye may be also" (John 14:1-3).*

That's the kind of elder Brother you have and *that's* the kind of God our Father is!

As children of the living God, we have an inheritance that is *"eternal under the heavens" (2 Corinthians 5:1)*. It is God-given, and no one can take it from us. So, don't walk around as if you have no hope, and nothing for which to look forward. *With God, there is always hope.* Child of God, you are an heir and joint-heir with

Jesus! Walk humbly before Him. You have good things coming in the natural world and greater things in the world to come. Trust God. The best is yet to come!

> **Affirmation #3: "You are an heir according to the promise that God gave Abraham."**
>
> *"And if ye [be] Christ's, then are ye Abraham's seed, and heirs according to the promise."*
>
> Galatians 3:29

Your assignment: Think out of the box, i.e., expand your mind beyond your normal thinking. In your journal, make a list of the intangible things (things that you cannot see, but know are available to you) that God has given you *personally* since you believed. Once you have completed your list, thank God for His marvelous gifts to you. Then watch the blessings that come forth out of your praise.

Journal   Date_____

CHAPTER 5

"Ye Are the Light of the World"

"Ye are the light of the world. A city that is set on an hill cannot be hid. Neither do men light a candle and put it under a bushel but on a candlestick; and it giveth light unto all that are in the house. Let you light so shine before men, that they may see your good works, and glorify your Father which is in heaven" (Matthew 5:14-16).

Unlike the natural world, the spiritual world has always had light. That is because it has always had God *(In the beginning God"... Genesis 1:1).* The Bible book of 1 John attests to the spiritual truth that God is light:

> *"This then is the message we have heard of him, and declare unto you, that GOD IS LIGHT, and in him is no darkness at all" (1 John 1:5, capitalized for emphasis).*

The psalmist David also knew God to be light: *The Lord is my LIGHT and my salvation; whom shall I fear? The Lord is the strength of my life; of whom shall I be afraid?" (Psalm 27:1, capitalization mine).* The Lord is the Author of who I am.

God the Creator spoke light into existence: *"And God said, Let there be light: and there was light" (Genesis 1:3).* His purpose was to dispel the darkness, even that which *"was on the face of the deep" (Genesis 1:2).*

We know that light illuminates, uncovers or exposes. Light gives off heat, and radiates from the one true God. God's light reveals and helps us see a thing (even things that pertains to ourselves) that is covered by darkness. What is God's light? His light is His word. The psalmist said: *"Thy WORD is a lamp unto my feet, and a light unto my path" (Psalm 119:105, capitalization mine).* God's light in the form of His word, assists us to see circumstances, storms, stumbling blocks, that are "in our way" or placed in our way, so that we can avoid, go through, or circumvent them safely and stay on the right path.

Spiritual darkness represents sin, wickedness and every evil work. Evil brings with it ignorance or spiritual blindness, a stubborn and closed mind, and half-truths (still lies) that easily contribute to the development of faulty thinking patterns and attitudes.

When we sin, light in the form of "the truth of God's word" exposes our sins. This exposure's purpose is to uncover the detrimental "hidden things of the heart". When light exposes the sins that we have committed and thought we had covered, it enables us to see the need to confess, repent (turn away) and advance to the next level in our spiritual growth through obedience to God. That is why it is so important that we study God's word. It is the measuring stick that helps us discern whether our "conversation" (the way we live) is right before God. Also, reading God's word will lead us to His Son. We will soon discover that Jesus is the light that we must follow:

> *"Then spake Jesus again unto them, saying, I AM THE LIGHT OF THE WORLD: he that followeth me shall not walk in darkness, but shall have the light of life" (John 8:12-capitalization mine).*

Just as the light in the wilderness represented God's presence among the people, Jesus' light represents His abiding presence with those who accept Him as Savior. He clearly gives the reason for following in verse 29 of the same chapter, as recorded in the Amplified Bible:

> *"And He who sent Me is ever with Me: My Father has not left me alone, FOR I ALWAYS DO WHAT PLEASES HIM" (John 8:29, capitalized for emphasis).*

Jesus said that just as His Father was ever with Him, so would He be with us. To that we can recognize an added bonus: When we truly commit to following Jesus, there is no mistake about whether or not we are doing the things that are pleasing in God's sight, for Jesus said that He always does what pleases God. Following Jesus will lead us to do the same. When we allow Jesus' light to shine forth in our lives, we have nothing to fear:

> *"The LORD is my light and my salvation; whom shall I fear? the LORD is the strength of my life; of whom shall I be afraid"(Psalm 27:1).*

Jesus becomes our light. He is the standard by which you "see" with your spiritual eyes. Jesus also becomes your salvation. He is the One who looks out for our welfare and prospers us. Jesus is the One who strengthens, protects us, and gives us victory. There is no need to fear darkness when we make the LORD our light. Thus, as Christians, we must keep Jesus as the center of our life, and let all things emanate from *His* light within us.

Christians must also know that following Jesus is a daily process:

> *"And Jesus said to them all, If any man will come after me, let him deny himself, and take up his cross daily, and follow me" (Luke 9:23).*

Whatever He did, we are to do. Wherever He went, we are to go. We are to allow His light to shine abroad in our hearts, and when we do so, it then radiates out to others. The "others" include anyone with whom we come in contact (our "neighbors"), and especially those in our sphere of influence, who by our "conversation" i.e., the way we live, will take notice and see Jesus in us. The ultimate aim of the light that we have been given is to bring glory to God the Father by showing the way to Christ Jesus, i.e., drawing others to God's Son.

Be it known that the light that we have in Jesus will have a powerful effect on us as well. Exposure to it will not allow us to remain the same. It will bring about a spiritual renewal of our minds, causing us to refocus our priorities and attitudes, and the work that we must do to advance God's kingdom by witnessing to others. Jesus' light means that we cannot operate in the "darkness" of an ignorant and closed mind, but must be willing to be "led by the Spirit", i.e., we must put our own agendas down, become obedient, and follow God's guidelines.

> "For as many as are led by the Spirit of God, they are
> the sons of God" (Romans 8:14).

Realize that the light that is within you will not allow you to think that you can act any way you please, say anything you want to say, manipulate anyone you want to your advantage, and get away with it. When you are truly in Christ Jesus, the Holy Spirit that lives within you will convict your spirit toward repentance rather than allow you to manipulate Him (which is something you cannot do anyway). Because you are a born-again Christian, you have been called out of darkness (a state of spiritual ignorance) to be different and to make a difference in the world. Your lives should show that you are indeed "peculiar" (different from the world's norm):

> "But ye are a chosen generation, a royal priesthood,
> an holy nation, a peculiar people; that ye should shew
> forth the praises of him who hath called you out of
> darkness into his marvellous light" (1 Peter 2:9).

When the world sees you, they will be drawn to you because you are not like everyone else. You are like Jesus. You can see then that you are very valuable to God and were given your light to show forth His praises-to bring honor and praises to His name: *"Ye are the light of the world..." (Matthew 5:14a).*

If your light is not producing *"whatsoever things are true, honest, just, pure, lovely and of a good report" (Philippians 4:8 paraphrased),* you may need to re-examine yourself to see if you have strayed away from the lighted path that God has planned for you. If you find that you have, then, get back on track. The God who is light will help you do that through the power of the Holy Spirit that lives in you.

Another reason to let your light shine is that your light exposes to the world the evil works of the Devil. One thing that he does not like is to have a saint pull the covers off the evil strategies he has planned for God's children. That is why he tries so hard to destroy our Christian testimony. The saying is true then that darkness and light have no dealings with each other (John 1:5). The darkness can try but it cannot extinguish something that it does not understand. It has no power to extinguish the light that God has created.

There are times that we allow "things" (trials, circumstances, situations, our emotions, and persecutions) to block our light by allowing them to take precedence in our lives. They take "center stage". We worry about them daily. We talk about them daily. As a result, they steal our focus and cause us to place that focus on the things that we are experiencing rather than on God's ability to deliver us. We must remember that there is not a situation that we have gone through, are going through, or will ever go through that God does not already know about. God is a God who is *always* in control. We often grieve the Holy Spirit by letting trials, circumstances, persecutions, and other "things" block our light as we go and have our own "pity party". When we come to ourselves and realize what we have done, often we are ashamed to confess to the Holy Spirit that we know we have grieved Him. Child of God, He already knows but wants us to get these "issues" out into the open so that He can show us how to deal with them, resolve them-then move on. The Holy Spirit will teach us to clean up our act and remove the barriers that block our light so that it can shine. Our lives will become that "city upon a hill" which gives "light" so that all can see the path to Jesus.

The book of Ephesians sums up the influence of our light:

> *"For though your hearts were once full of darkness, now you are full of light from the Lord, and your behavior should show it! For this light within you produces only what is good and right and true"* *(Ephesians 5:8-9)* <u>Life Application Study Bible,</u> *New Living Translation, 1996.*

You are the light that shines in this world. You represent Jesus' physical presence in the earth. You already know that you are: *"in the midst of a crooked and perverse nation, among whom ye shine as lights in the world" (Philippians 2:15).* Allow your light to shine so that the "world" can see Jesus our Savior, and come running to Him! The brightness of your light is up to you: Go forth and shine!

Affirmation #4: "The Lord is your light and salvation."

> *"But if we walk in the light, as he is in the light, we have fellowship one with another, and the blood of Jesus Christ his Son cleanseth us from all sin." 1 John 1:7.*

You have a light and a legacy in Christ Jesus.

Your assignment: *"Think on these things…about your "light" and your "legacy".* Generally speaking, a legacy is a positive or negative influence that is passed on from one generation to the next. A positive legacy in human beings could be a propensity toward being freehearted or giving. On the other hand, a negative legacy could be the inclination to be stingy and tight-fisted, keeping everything for yourself. Be honest as you journal the answers to the following questions.

- Has someone you know or someone in your family line passed on a negative legacy to you that would cause your light to dim?
- What is that legacy (trait(s)?
- How has it hindered you from fully performing your calling to be the "light of the world"?
- What do you want God to change about you that will make your light shine brighter?

Journal   Date_____

CHAPTER 6

Ambassadors for Christ

"Now then we are ambassadors for Christ, as God did beseech you by us; we pray you in Christ's stead, be ye reconciled to God" (2 Corinthians 5:20).

As he spoke the above words to the church at Corinth, the apostle Paul explained a believer's work in the ministry as being an "ambassador" or representative of Christ. *The Merriam Webster Online Dictionary* defines an "ambassador" as "an official envoy; an authorized representative or messenger." In spiritual terms, an ambassador is one who is authorized by God through Jesus Christ to be his messenger and/or spokesperson. An ambassadors' ultimate aim is to proclaim the message of the gospel to anyone who will hear it.

It is a given that we as Christians do perform many functions and have many gifts and talents by which we can serve in the body of Christ. We may serve inside our local church as pastors, deacons, teachers, ushers, greeters, musicians, and in many other service capacities. Yet, it is also true that one of our major roles is to represent Christ wherever we go. In our daily walk as Christians, we are to be "ambassadors for Christ" just as was the apostle Paul and his spiritual contemporaries. An ambassador is a calling that every Christian shares. You have been sent! (Matthew 28:19-20).

As ambassadors, we must pay particular attention not to step out of bounds by acting on our own. Our authorization as ambassadors comes from Jesus Himself, and is embodied in the Scripture commonly referred to as "The Great Commission":

> "Go ye therefore, and teach all nations, baptizing them in the mane of the Father, and of the son, and of the Holy Ghost: Teaching them to observe all things whatsoever I have commanded you: and, lo I am with you always, even unto the end of the world" (Matthew 28:19-20).

We are to say what God through the Holy Spirit tells us to say. We are authorized representatives sent by Jesus to spread the gospel of peace and reconciliation to a world that is lost in sin. In other words, our job is to lead sinners to Christ, to exhort or give encouragement, and use our spiritual gifts to edify our sisters and brothers who are in the body of Christ.

In his role as an "ambassador", the apostle Paul admonished members of the Corinthian church to be reconciled, i.e., to re-establish their relationship with God by returning to holy living and to the sound doctrinal foundation that had been laid out for them through wholesome teaching. In essence, Paul was saying "You cannot represent God when you live the way you have always lived." Straddling the fence will not do. Being a "crowd pleaser" will not do. You are not to go along with what you know is not right so that you may be popular or accepted of men. You are not to turn to the left or the right (no compromise) when you encounter issues in this world. Whatever God says about the subject is where you must stand, even if you must stand alone. God does not change:

"⁶ For I am the LORD, *I change not;..." (Malachi 3:6), and "God is not man that He should lie" (Numbers 23:19).*

What God said was an abomination to Him then, is an abomination now. What was truth then is truth now. Ask Him to show you how to respond in love to the current and pressing issues of this world.

As you live, you will find that there are some immature Christians that have faulty thinking patterns regarding Jesus' command to "Go ye into all the world..." We think that when Jesus made this command, He was thinking not of us but about those other "spiritual" folk. You know, the "ones" in that *other* church or that other neighborhood, or even that other denomination. That is because we have closed our hearts to those who are lost and in need of the very thing that we now have-eternal life. We have become desensitized to suffering and the needs of others. Our focus on the things of God has shifted and our major emphasis has turned toward ourselves. "I've got mine. Let somebody else do it. I'm too busy." Yes, we serve as deacons or Sunday school teachers, or choir members, in the church nursery, in the Children's church ministry, as ushers or greeters, or in some other auxiliary. These are indeed noble ways to give our service to the body of believers.

Yet, we have not stopped to consider those who are our brothers and sisters in other churches, *or* those who are nonbelievers and therefore on their way to hell. They are the lost ones after whom we must seek. Oh, we do our little "service" here and there. We go through our closets and hand out a few clothes that we can no longer wear. Then we think that "they" ought to be grateful. But what about carrying the news of the gospel of Jesus Christ to those who are outside the walls of the church? We say: "I am going to pray about whether the Lord wants me to get involved in another ministry. I'm already doing a lot for the church." We conveniently forget that God is concerned not only for those who are already in the body of Christ (not the church building) but especially for those who are not. We have become presumptuous in thinking that God will be satisfied if we do just enough to get by. We have forgotten that God is not a respecter of persons (Romans 2:11) and is thus not willing that *any* should perish:

> *"The Lord is not slack concerning his promise, as some men count slackness; but is longsuffering to us-ward, not willing that any should perish, but that all should come to repentance" (2 Peter 3:9).*

We seem to have gotten our priorities mixed up. Our first calling is to be obedient to God's word by doing what He has told us to do. For those who do "go", Jesus did not tell us to watch others and criticize what they are or are not doing. And He definitely did not commission us to be "accusers" of our own brothers and sisters in the body of Christ. There is great danger in that. When those in Christ do sin, or do something that may seem to be out of Christian character, we are more apt to say "Maybe he or she was not who *I* thought they were". That's judging, and God said that we are not to participate in judging others:

> *"¹Judge not, that ye be not judged.² For with what judgment ye judge, ye shall be judged: and with what measure ye mete, it shall be measured to you again" (Matthew 7:1-2).*

We were not perfect when God accepted us; and we certainly are not perfect now. He took us just as we were. Prayer and empathy for that person would be more in order. As Christians, sometimes we are the first to take a stab at tearing down another Christian's character. In fact, sometimes we beat the Devil to it by allowing him to prod us on based on what someone else has said. The book of Romans 15:7 (New Living Translation) says:

> *"Therefore, accept each other just as Christ has accepted you so that God will be given glory."*

What glory can we gain for God by tearing someone else down? It's not our glory that we're seeking, or how we *feel* about God's saints. It is God's glory that we should be seeking by remembering how He accepted *us* with all of our faults and flaws. Jesus' commission is for us to go and minister to others *inside* and *outside* of the body of Christ.

Though our commission is to go forth and spread the gospel message, Jesus leads us to know that we are never alone. We have Jesus, and we have been sent the presence of the Holy Spirit-who sticks closer than a brother, and who gives us the power, wisdom and knowledge needed to accomplish the mission we have been sent to complete. Remember also that God will never send us anywhere ill-equipped.

As we carry out our daily activities, we all have a "sphere of influence", i.e., a time and place when we daily touch the lives of people that are not touched by other co-workers, family, friends and associates. Even though we may work in a large organization, attend a large school, etc., chances are great that we will not see everyone each day. But, we can do as the songwriter said: *"Brighten the Corner Where You Are"*. We can make that "little space" where we work a better place, because that is what we have been sent there to do.

We may not be able to pull out a Bible and show a scripture in certain situations, but we can live our lives in such a way that we draw people to Christ. We can keep our "spiritual ears and eyes" open to the leading of the Holy Spirit so that we will be able to discern when we are to be quiet and just listen, when we are to pray, when we are to speak, or when we are to give encouragement.

The gospel of Christ is not to be hidden but shared abroad. Our commission is to "tell it" wherever we go. We are not to force it upon others or pound it down their throats, as it were, but to recognize and seize every opportunity that presents itself (just as did the apostle Paul) to "preach the gospel". We are to listen to the voice of the Holy Spirit when He tells us: "Now is the time. Tell them this…" When we are obedient to Christ's commission, God will do the rest.

As an ambassador for Christ, our commission is to go into all the world. We may not be able to travel around the world, but we can tell those with whom we work, and those we see on a daily basis about Jesus and the things that He has done for us. We can testify of His ability to save them just as He saved us. We can testify of the great future and hope that is available for all who trust in Christ Jesus. Remember also that if we cannot travel, another way to tell the good news is to support, through monetary gifts and contributions, the ministries of others who do. This support however, does not come at the expense of our own church. *We are to pay our tithes and offerings at our own church!*

You are an ambassador for Christ. Jesus gave all Christians a commission to work in His Kingdom. Child of God, go and do as He has commanded.

Affirmation #5: You are a partaker of God's marvelous light.

"But ye [are] a chosen generation, a royal priesthood, an holy nation, a peculiar people; that ye should shew forth the praises of him who hath called you out of darkness into his marvellous light:" 1 Peter 2:9.

Your assignment: In your journal, tell of a time when you acted as an ambassador for Christ. To whom did you witness? Were you satisfied with the results? Given another opportunity (and it will come), what would you do differently?

Journal   Date_____

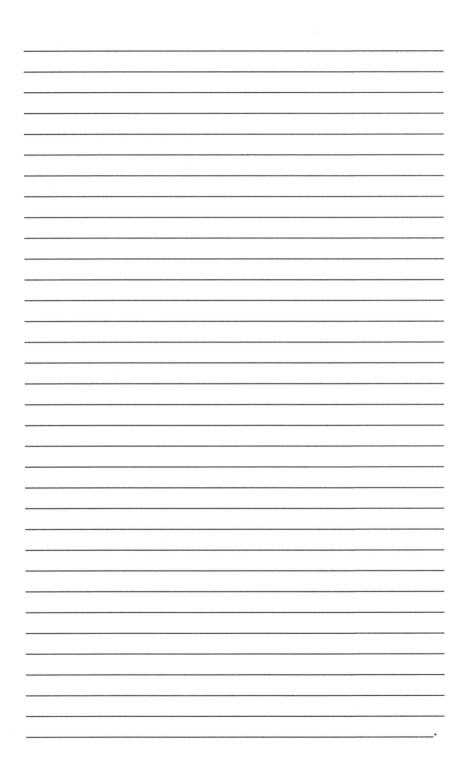

CHAPTER 7

"You Are the Salt of the Earth"

Ye are the salt of the earth: but if the salt have lost his savour, wherewith shall it be salted? it is thenceforth good for nothing, but to be cast out, and to be trodden under foot of men (Matthew 5:13).

As in today's economy, salt was an extremely important commodity during Bible times. It was used as a seasoning, a food preservative, and an agent to cure animal hides. Salt was also used to heal wounds, and prevent mildew. In fact, salt had a few out of the ordinary uses. In the book of Judges, Abimelech salted the ground after he had defeated his enemies in the town of Shechem (Judges 9:45). This spoiled the soil so that it would no longer be good for producing crops.

As relates to the Roman government, it is said that salt was also a part of the salary of a Roman soldier. Salt also had its importance in the daily sacrifices of the early Israelites. In Leviticus 2:13, God required that salt be added to every meat offering. As recorded in the Internet-based *WebBible Encyclopedia,* a meat offering "followed the sacrifice of blood, and consisted of "flour or cakes prepared in a special way with oil and frankincense"[7] and was offered on a daily basis with the burnt offering.

Another important aspect of salt had to do with what was known as the "covenant of salt":

> *"As salt was regarded as a necessary ingredient of the daily food, and of all sacrifices offered to Yahweh, it became an easy step to the very close connection between salt and covenant making. When men ate together, they became friends. Compare the Arabic expression, "There is salt between us". "He has eaten of my salt", which means partaking of hospitality that cemented friendship...Covenants were generally confirmed by sacrificial meals and salt was always present. Since, too, salt was a preservative, it would easily become symbolic of an enduring covenant. David received his kingdom forever through a covenant of salt (2 Chronicles 13:5)."[8]*

During the Sermon on the Mount, Jesus used salt as a description of His followers:

> *"Ye are the salt of the earth: but if the salt have lost his savour, wherewith shall it be salted? It is thenceforth good for nothing, but to be cast out, and to be trodden of men" (Matthew 5:13).*

Jesus used salt as an example because He knew that all of the people could relate to the value and necessity of salt as a seasoning agent and preservative. They could also identify with His description because most knew of at least one famous story in the Bible concerning salt (Lot's wife turned into a pillar of salt).

Jesus said that we as Christians should have a positive spiritual influence on those with whom we come in contact, whether Christian or non-Christian. In other words, we are to make a positive and lasting difference in the lives of others. When the world looks at us, they should see a reflection of Jesus. When they come in contact with us, they should not feel worse when they leave, but should have found courage, edification, encouragement, strength to persevere, and a greater awareness of the truth that is found in God's word. If we as Christians do not have an impact on those with whom we live, we are on the verge of "losing our savor", our ability to be useful and effective witnesses for Christ. We must provide Christians and non-Christians with the things that are necessary to live in this world without being "of the world." It is our responsibility to be "potent" witnesses of the hope that is in Jesus as Lord and Savior.

We can also lose our savor when we say that we are salt yet continue in the ways of the world. We cannot afford to "lay our religion down" when we get upset, go and curse our neighbors, and then pick it back up after we've finished the job. We cannot be a participant in road rage, and then act like saints when we arrive home. We cannot gossip about our sisters and brothers in Christ, and then hide our hands as if *we* are innocent. One "little" sin is just as bad as a "big" sin. God requires clean hands and a pure heart from all of us. The salt that we are signifies a true calling to share a rare and precious gift, a gift that sustains. That gift comes in the person of Jesus Christ-a most precious "Pearl" without price. We must therefore be careful to guard our "testimony" so that we can be of value to others. The world is watching. More importantly, the devil is cunningly watching to seize any opportunity we leave open so that he can advance his evil cause. He will seek to steal and destroy our salt. Satan would like nothing better than for us to stray, and become limp, weak Christians so that he can step in and destroy our Christian witness. He wants us to "lose our savor", i.e., our value to the work of God. Thus, in all that we do, we must watch and pray that we not be ignorant of his evil devices nor yield to him, but truly be the potent and flavorful "salt" that seasons the lives of others and truly represents Jesus Christ.

Affirmation # 6: "You were chosen and ordained by God."

> *"Ye have not chosen me, but I have chosen you, and ordained you, that ye should go and bring forth fruit, and [that] your fruit should remain: that whatsoever ye shall ask of the Father in my name, he may give it you." John 15:16*

Your assignment: There are many times when we have opportunities to be "salt" but miss doing so because of our own shortcomings. Be honest with yourself. Write in your journal and tell of a time when you did not act as "salt" to a non-believer, or a believer. How did they react? Did you attempt to do anything to make it right? If so, what did you do? If you decided to do nothing, what was your reasoning? If you had a second chance, (God is a God of second, third, fourth, etc., chances) how would you handle the situation this time?

Journal   Date_____

CHAPTER 8

"We are More than Conquerors". We are Overcomers!

"Who shall separate us from the love of Christ? shall tribulation, or distress, or persecution, or famine, or nakedness, or peril, or sword? As it is written, For thy sake we are killed all the day long; we are accounted as sheep for the slaughter. Nay, in all these things we are more than conquerors through him that loved us. For I am persuaded, that neither death, nor life, nor angels, nor principalities, nor powers, nor things present, nor things to come, Nor height, nor depth, nor any other creature, shall be able to separate us from the love of God, which is in Christ Jesus our Lord (Romans 8:35-39).

According to *Merriam Webster's Dictionary Online*, a conqueror "gains control over situations and people by surmounting impediments. He or she subdues and thus gains a decisive victory".[9] Our enemy the Devil, would have us believe that we cannot and will not overcome or win in this life. He does not want us to "finish our course", and we already know that he is a liar (John 8:44).

One of the ways that we can know that we are victorious through life's trials, is by reading and acknowledging through the Scriptures, the victories that God has given to his saints. When we look at the lives of Abraham, Moses, Joshua, Esther, Ruth, Job, Joseph, Daniel, countless other saints, and most definitely of our Lord and Savior Jesus Christ, we learn that God has placed their biographies i.e., their life stories in His word as examples of victorious living. We can definitely apply them to our own lives. Looking at the lives of these saints lets us know that we can have that same victory. In fact, victory is already ours.

A great strategy of the Devil is to make us believe that we are defeated before we get started. His aim is to try and separate us from God by enticing and tempting us to lose hope, and turn to sin as we try to work thing out *our* way. He already knows the devastation of being separated from God's love and would like nothing better than to have Christians share in his misery. Thus, he will use even the things that the Scriptures say we would suffer in order to prevent us from reaching God's goals for us. His goal is to weaken our defenses. Our enemy will use:

> ➤ Tribulation (just plain trouble);
> ➤ Distress (upset brought on by agitation, alarm, and/or discomfort);
> ➤ Calamity (catastrophe, disaster, tragedy);
> ➤ Confinement (bondage or addictions, physical or emotional imprisonment);
> ➤ Disability (physical, mental, cognitive, or developmental impairment);
> ➤ Anguish (misery that causes heartache, loss of joy, distress or torment);
> ➤ Physical or mental oppression (sometimes both, and at the same time); Persecution (aggravation, irritation, exasperation so that his continuous pressure may cause us to make a hasty decisions in any given situation) and harassment (persistent annoyance);

➤ Famine (physical hunger, financial scarcity, or lack);

➤ Nakedness (He will attempt to expose, bare, disgrace, blemish or tarnish our reputations and our spiritual testimony; and even put us in spiritual rags);

➤ Perils (Satan will use any difficulties or dangers to put us at risk). He will even use the threat of *death (See the book of Job)* to frighten us and try and make us feel that God has abandoned us.

The Scriptures are very clear about this fact:

"...we wrestle not against flesh and blood, but against principalities, against powers, against the rulers of the darkness of this world, against spiritual wickedness in high places" (Ephesians 6:12).

Satan plays "mind games" with our thoughts by orchestrating situations designed to cause us (if possible) to panic and lose our very sanity. He even has demons assigned to weaken our faith. He wants us to continue to ask God *"why*?*"*. That is the reason it is so important after *"having done all, stand"* on His word. God alone is always faithful.

The psalmist said:

"If it had not been the LORD who was on our side, when men rose up against us: Then they had swallowed us up quick, when their wrath was kindled against us: Then the waters had overwhelmed us, the stream had gone over our soul: Then the proud waters had gone over our soul. : Blessed be the LORD, who hath not given us as a prey to their teeth. Our soul is escaped as a bird out of the snare of the fowlers: the snare is broken, and we are escaped. Our help is in the name of the Lord who made heaven and earth" (Psalm 124:2-8).

We are not alone. God has not given us over to Satan's teeth, neither has He given us over to the hands of mere mortal men. When God lifts up a standard against our enemies (Isaiah 59:19) and fights for us, you had better believe that His power is devastating to those powers, principalities, rulers of darkness, and any other evil spirits that are organized against us and seeking to annihilate us! When God lifts up a standard against our enemies all that see it will know that God has us under His protection. God's standard or banner over us in essence says: "They are mine! I will fight for them!" It is then time for our enemies to retreat, or be annihilated themselves!

Besides that, the Holy Scriptures states that through faith in Christ Jesus, we are already over-comers:

> *"For whatsoever is born of God overcometh the world;*
> *and this is the victory that overcometh the world, even*
> *our faith" (I John 5:4).*

There are many examples and accounts in the Bible of saints who have faced the perils of life (and death), and have been victorious. One such example in the book of Judges, chapters 6-8, is Gideon. Gideon is a good choice for an over-comer because he was a man who represents the character of many Christians today. They know that they have a calling upon their lives, but because they have a poor self-image, i.e., think so little of themselves, and often who others say that they are, they suffer from low self-esteem. This makes them unaware of their actual strength in God, and sometimes closes the door to any action on their part.

When we take our first look at Gideon, he is threshing grain at the bottom of a winepress on his father's property trying to keep from being discovered by the Midianites. Earlier, God had delivered the Israelites into the hands of the Midianites because they had turned their back on Him and had begun to worship the idols of the nations around them. They did this even after they had been warned on several occasions against doing so.

The Midianites were cruel taskmasters. They devastated the country and almost succeeded in literally starving the Israelites to death. Though the Israelites were disobedient, they were still God's chosen. Their cries moved Him to act on their behalf.

There is Gideon in the winepress being hailed by an angel of the Lord: *"And the angel of the Lord appeared unto him, and said unto him, The Lord is with thee, thou mighty man of valour" (Judges 6:12).*

Notice that he is not at all in awe at the presence of this divine entity. He does not bow, nor does he show any kind of humility. He seemingly has no time for a divine visitation. Gideon has his own earthly troubles and sorrows with which to deal. Securing enough grain to feed his starving family weighs heavily on his mind. Aside from that, the continued oppression of his people is a major nagging concern.

When the angel greets him as a mighty man of valor, Gideon, by his expression, seems not to be aware of his own innate abilities. He responds with a tirade of bitterness and disbelief at how the Israelites are being treated:

> *"And Gideon said unto him, Oh my Lord, if the Lord be with us, why then is all this befallen us? And where are all his miracles which our fathers told us of, saying, Did not the Lord bring us up from Egypt? but now the Lord hath forsaken us, and delivered us into the hands of the Midianites" (Judges 6:13).*

"Poor us" he seems to say. He has missed the point. God has chosen and commanded him to "save Israel from the hand of the Midianites", yet Gideon thinks only of himself and what he cannot do:

> *"And he said unto him, Oh my Lord, wherewith shall I save Israel? Behold, my family is poor in Mannasseh, and I am the least in my father's house" (Judges 6:15).*

Imagine what his response would sound like in this day: "Who me? Are you calling me a mighty man of valor? You certainly could not be talking to me. *My family is poor...and I am the least in my father's house. I am a nobody. I have nothing to work with.*" Gideon could not believe that God would call upon a self-perceived weakling like himself to deliver Israel from their enemies.

We see him later still unsure of what he has heard as he asks God for a sign. Gideon thinks: *"God I heard what you said, but I still doubt if you want to use someone like me. If you really want me to deliver Israel as you say I will, show me a sign. When I see it with my own eyes, then I will believe that I have truly been called to be this leader and do this great work."* Even though God's anger is kindled against Gideon, He gives him the signs he requests.

Gideon is definitely insecure, fearful and suffers from issues of low self-esteem. He is not at all sure of himself. However, one good thing is also true about him; once he becomes satisfied with God's answer, he is obedient to God's call even though he is afraid. This shows great, albeit hidden strength in character. God knew from the beginning that there was something in Gideon with which He could work.

Sometimes, we as Christians hear God's call but are afraid to act. We are afraid of what our friends, spouses, family, and even our spiritual leaders might think about our calling. Realistically, this calling has nothing "spiritually" to do with them. It is between God and us. This is often the case, especially if we are women with a calling upon our lives. We have allowed ourselves to be held back for so long. We have closed our ears to what God has told us to do and have sought to satisfy everybody else-but God. As women, we have relegated ourselves to "speaking on the back of the bus." We are afraid to speak that word that God has told us to speak because we become afraid of what *"they"* might say to or about us or how *"they"* might change their perception of us. Yet, how often have we heard it said that *"they"* do not have a heaven or a hell in which to put us? God has already commanded us to *"seek Him first"*. It is not important for us to have the approval of any man [or woman] to do what God tells us to do.

We may not have thought about the fact that even if women may not have a great influence on men, women can impact and reach other women in a way in which men may not be able to. We have a "sisterhood" that enables us to explain to each other our plight, and empathize with given situations. We have a ministry of encouragement among each other that reaches deep into the heart.

God wants to see if we (men and women) are willing to be obedient and faithful to what *He* has told us to do, despite our shaky opinion of ourselves, and regardless of the opinions of others. God wants to show ordinary people that they can be extraordinary by being obedient and faithful to *His* calling.

Finally, we have to rid ourselves of the notion that when we as women (and men) are called to do and speak what *"thus saith the Lord"* it is necessary to stand in a pulpit to do it. God wants us to be bold enough to speak for Him wherever we are, and where they let us stand.

As we complete the biblical account of Gideon, we find that despite his shortcomings, God orchestrated his success in defeating the Midianites. With God's help and only three hundred men, Gideon defeated an army of thousands, and he used that which was ordinary and of common use.

The Bible also tells us that with the same strength in character and with the aid of the Holy Spirit, we as God's sons and daughters can defeat any entity, evil spirit, or circumstance that seeks to separate us from our God, destroy our testimony, and negate His calling on our lives. We are commanded to be obedient to His calling knowing that nothing can separate us from His love:

> *"For I am persuaded, that neither death, nor life, nor angels, nor principalities, nor powers, nor things present, nor things to come, nor height, nor depth, nor any other creature, shall be able to separate us from*

*the love of God, which is in Christ Jesus our Lord
(Romans 8:38-39).*

Like Gideon, we can be victorious when faced with overwhelming odds. We need to be ever mindful of the fact that with Christ's help we can do all things (Philippians 4:13). We must then faithfully work and abide until Jesus returns. We have been called to be over-comers! Let's shout for victory now!

Affirmation # 7: You are neither a weakling nor a wimp. In Christ Jesus, you are an over-comer! God already knows this because He knew you and had a plan for you before you were in your mother's womb.

"Before I formed thee in the belly I knew thee; and before thou camest forth out of the womb, I sanctified thee, [and] I ordained thee a prophet unto the nations. " Jeremiah 1:5;

"For I know the thoughts that I think toward you, saith the LORD, thoughts of peace, and not of evil, to give you an expected end." Jeremiah 29:11

Your assignment: Choose one of these Bible Characters: Daniel, David, Esther, Job, Joseph, Paul, Ruth... (Or choose one of your own). Read about your choice in the Bible. Then write in your journal and tell why you think that he/she was more than a conqueror. Back up your answer with Scripture. How can you use this example in your current situation? Also, give an example of a trial or tribulation that you have gone through, and tell how the Lord delivered you.

Journal   Date_____

CHAPTER 9

Your Body: The Temple of the Holy Ghost

"Know ye not that ye are the temple of God and that the Spirit of God dwelleth in you? If any man defile the temple of God, him shall God destroy; for the temple of God is holy, which temple ye are"(1 Corinthians, chapter 3:16-17).

In Bible times, the temple was more than merely a place of worship. For the Israelites, it represented the presence of God among His people. Therefore, the temple was deemed a holy *house of the Lord* (I Kings 6:17). Other terms used for the temple included: *the house of my glory* (Isaiah 60:7), a *house of prayer* (Matthew 21:13), *the palace for the Lord God*, (I Chronicles 29:1). Jesus called the temple *my Father's house* (John 2:16).

Did you know that you do not own yourself? The Scriptures say: "your body is the temple of the Holy Ghost": Therefore, you are not your own, but God's temple:

"What? Know ye not that your body is the temple of the Holy Ghost which is in you, which ye have of God, and ye are not your own?" (I Corinthians 6:19).

Your body then is made so that God's Spirit can dwell in it. Thus, we are not to defile the temple in which God's Spirit dwells. We are not to morally or physically pollute or contaminate, or corrupt our bodies. There are many ways to defile our temple. Galatians 5:19-21 says:

"Now the works of the flesh are manifest, which are these; Adultery, fornication, uncleanness, lasciviousness, 20": Idolatry, witchcraft, hatred, variance, emulations, wrath, strife, seditions, heresies, envyings, murders, drunkenness, revellings, and such like: of the which I tell you before, as I have also told you in time past, that they which do such things shall not inherit the kingdom of God."

We can defile our temple by giving our mind over to "the works" of the flesh. That means we allow the natural self to rule what we do with our spiritual bodies thus turning it into something that is unholy or unclean-a place where the Holy Spirit is grieved to dwell. We allow our "flesh" to influence what we think, and eventually what we do.

There are many addictions in this world that seem to be insurmountable. These addictions begin subtly as urges to placate some perceived need, emotion, or desire, and mushrooms in later life into demons that are uncontrollable and unwholesome. Some have been attempting for years to release themselves from all kinds of hellish dilemmas.

Often, the answer has already been deposited inside of us. When we confessed Jesus as our Savior, He sent us a Comforter whose function was and is to teach us to deal with the everyday problems that confront us:

"But the Comforter, which is the Holy Ghost, whom the Father will send in my name, he shall teach you all things, and bring all things to your remembrance, whatsoever I have said unto you"(John 14:26).

That comforter is the Person of the Holy Spirit. If we will be entirely honest with ourselves, we will admit that the Holy Spirit has already spoken with us regarding the unholy habits (whatever they are) in which we find ourselves entangled. The trouble is that we have failed to listen. We have felt more comfortable listening to another voice. It told us that we could continue to do what we were doing, and when the time was right, the world would find an easy solution to help us get out of our self-induced situation. We have been waiting for the world to invent a "panacea- a cure all" which would allow us to meet all of our desires and then take a little pill and solve the problem. If that did not work, we thought that we were smart enough to find a solution on our own. In the meantime, as we made this alliance with our flesh, we allowed ourselves to sink deeper and deeper into the problem. We seem to have no desire to relinquish our "comfort zone".

We realized (almost too late) that the voice that we heard (It's all right to take care of your fleshly desires first", etc.) was not the voice of the Holy Spirit. This other voice isolated us from others and made us think that we were in control. It told us to close our ears to the godly advice or wise counsel of other Christians. This voice also loaded us with guilt. When we looked, we found that we were alone, the problem was still with us, had gotten a toehold, then a foothold, and had finally grown into a stronghold. Additionally, we were carrying around a bag full of guilt. We forgot that we could not fight this battle in our own strength. We forgot that there is nothing we can do apart from Jesus. He said so in John 15:5: "*...without me ye can do nothing.*"

We also have "silent or secret" sins we must deal with (the ones we try to hide so that others will not discover "the real us"). But, we can begin anew by repenting and confessing to God that we have messed up. Indeed, we have been disobedient to His word. Isaiah 1:19 tell us that if we are to eat the good of the land, we must be *"willing and obedient."* God will forgive us and show us that we can change. Indeed, He will fix the problems in us. We must learn to rely on Him even in our self-created, self-centered "mess". Finally, we must make a conscious effort to "think about what we are doing and what we're thinking about". We must intentionally be obedient to the still small voice that has spoken to us time and time again. Then, after being freed, we must not become entangled again.

The 8th chapter of Romans tells us that the flesh and the Spirit do not agree because they are constantly at war with each other. God tells us to "walk in the Spirit" because He knows that that is the easier way to subdue the flesh. We cannot go wrong when we listen and obey the voice of the Holy Spirit. The indwelling presence of the Holy Spirit will speak for us when we have no strength to speak for ourselves. Scriptures says this about the Holy Spirit:

> *"Likewise the Spirit also helpeth our infirmities: for we know not what we should pray for as we ought: but the Spirit itself maketh intercession for us with groanings which cannot be uttered. And he that searcheth the hearts knoweth what is the mind of the Spirit, because he maketh intercession for the saints according to the will of God. And we know that all things work together for good to them that love God, to them who are the called according to his purpose" (Romans 8:26-28).*

God wants us to be faithful in even the little things. Luke, chapter 16:10 states: *"He that is faithful in that which is least is faithful also in much: and he that is unjust in the least is unjust also in much".*

If we would focus on the fact that as Christians, our body does not belong to us, but is inhabited by the Holy Spirit, we might feel quite a bit different about things that we do that are detrimental to our physical and most especially spiritual temple. Our bodies are indeed the temple of the Holy Ghost, and as such are to be used only to bring glory to God. Our spiritual body needs the strength that we are giving to our physical body, i.e., we need to strengthen our stance in Jesus by feasting on His word. When we are fully satisfied, then we will thank God that He gave us a body that He cares about enough to inhabit! Your body is the temple of the Holy Spirit. Be proud of this and don't defile it. Appropriately, God tells us how to produce *fruit* that will assist others and benefit ourselves as well:

> [22] *But the fruit of the Spirit is love, joy, peace, longsuffering, gentleness, goodness, faith,* [23] *Meekness, temperance: against such there is no law"(Galatians 5:22-23).*

You must bring glory to Him and bless His name by doing that which is pleasing in His sight!

Affirmation # 8: No matter the circumstances, remember that you CAN do all things through Christ.

> *"I can do all things through Christ which strengtheneth me." Philippians 4:13*

> *"There hath no temptation taken you but such as is common to man: but God [is] faithful, who will not suffer you to be tempted above that ye are able; but will with the temptation also make a way to escape, that ye may be able to bear [it]."*

> *I Corinthians 10:13.*

Your Assignment: Ask God to show you what you need to do to conquer a pressing problem(s) in your life. Ask God to help you set goals for yourself, i.e., Lord, what do *You* want me to do? As you make your goals, list the activities that you must complete to accomplish them. Next, <u>follow the plan that God has set before you.</u> Be patient. Remember that it may take some time for you to meet your goals. When seeking to conquer any "issue", remember that you did not get in your present condition overnight. Thus, long-term solutions may just be that, long term and may not come instantly. You must work at it, little by little. Be aware that you have an enemy whose desire it is to see you fail. Don't help him along.

Use your journal to keep a log of any victory be it large or small. Continue to realize that God's word is true and is the measuring stick for your success. With God's help, you can do all things! Philippians 4:13.

Journal

Date_____

_____
_____
_____
_____
_____
_____
_____
_____
_____
_____
_____
_____
_____
_____
_____
_____
_____
_____
_____
_____
_____
_____
_____
_____
_____
_____
_____
_____
_____
_____

CHAPTER 10

"You Have Been Redeemed!"

Adam and Eve sinned in the Garden of Eden by breaking God's command. God explicitly told Adam not to eat of a certain fruit, or he would die:

> *"And the LORD God commanded the man, saying, Of every tree of the garden thou mayest freely eat: But of the tree of the knowledge of good and evil, thou shalt not eat of it: for in the day that thou eatest thereof thou shalt surely die" (Genesis 2:16-17).*

Adam and Eve disobeyed and found that even though God still loved them, He is indeed a God of His word. God continued to love mankind, but they brought punishment on themselves and all mankind through their sin of disobedience. Now banished from the garden and from sweet communion with God, how were they to find their way back to Him?

Amazingly, before the foundation of the world, God had already made provisions for the reconciliation of mankind to Himself. This provision came through His Son Jesus Christ:

"Forasmuch as ye know that ye were not redeemed with corruptible things, as silver and gold, from your vain conversation received by tradition from your fathers; But with the precious blood of Christ, as of a lamb without blemish and without spot: Who verily was foreordained before the foundation of the world, but was manifest in these last times for you, who by him do believe in God, that raised him up from the dead, and gave him glory; that your faith and hope might be in God" (1 Peter 1:18-21).

In his daily devotional of December 16 [2003], Pastor Charles Stanley of the world renowned *"Intouch Ministries"* had these words to say about our redemption:

"When we talk about God caring enough to rescue us, we immediately wonder what we are being saved from and why rescue is necessary. The purpose of God's rescue operation was to save us from the penalty of death inflicted on Adam and Eve because they chose to sin against God. When they fell, the fountainhead of the whole human race sinned against God and brought condemnation on themselves and everyone yet to be born. No matter how hard we try to be good, the biblical verdict is that "there is none who does good . . . not even one" (Romans 3:12). This means there is no one who does enough good in any way to be made acceptable to God."[10]

It is awesome to know that despite our sin status, and in spite of the fact that we can do nothing to *earn* our way back to God, He did not orchestrate our eternal demise. God loved us so much that He cared enough to plan our undeserved rescue before we even knew Him. Before we decided to give Him a thought, we were on His mind. The following scripture gives us a spiritual picture of how loving God is:

> *"But God commendeth his love toward us, in that, while we were yet sinners, Christ died for us. Much more then, being now justified by his blood, we shall be saved from wrath through him. For if, when we were enemies, we were reconciled to God by the death of his Son, much more, being reconciled, we shall be saved by his life" (Romans 5:8-10).*

Jesus' death brought us back into full fellowship with God. Our sin state brought on by the sin or Adam and Eve had made us aliens and indeed enemies of God:

> *"That at that time ye were without Christ, being aliens from the commonwealth of Israel, and strangers from the covenants of promise, having no hope, and without God in the world: But now in Christ Jesus ye who sometimes were far off are made nigh by the blood of Christ. For he is our peace, who hath made both one, and hath broken down the middle wall of partition between us; Having abolished in his flesh the enmity, even the law of commandments contained in ordinances; for to make in himself of twain one new man, so making peace; And that he might reconcile both unto God in one body by the cross, having slain the enmity thereby; (Ephesians 2:12-16).*

Jesus freed us from the sins that were detrimental to the survival of our very souls. Had we remained in our sins, we would have been destined for eternal damnation. God knew that at the end of sin is death. Nothing good can come of sin. Thus, God redeemed us from sin by granting us a gift that no mere man could give. He gave us the gift of eternal life through the death of His Son Jesus Christ:

"For the wages of sin is death; but the gift of God is eternal life through Jesus Christ our Lord" (Romans 6:23).

Most Christians know the familiar song, *"Jesus Paid It All"*. However, many Christians do not truly realize the things from which we were redeemed. Through Jesus' death and resurrection, we have been made free from the condemnation that sin brings, free from anxiety, free from bondage, and free from the hands of the enemy. In addition, there were other benefits that belong to us based on God's gift of His Son. Here are a few of them:

- ➢ We were redeemed from the curse of death and the grave, and granted eternal life.
  (Hosea 13:14). "I will ransom them from the power of the grave; I will redeem them from death: O death, I will be thy plagues; O grave, I will be thy destruction: repentance shall be hid from mine eyes." Psalm 49:15 – "But God will redeem my soul from the power of the grave: for he shall receive me. Selah."
- ➢ We were redeemed from hell, and given an eternal home in heaven: *Psalm 86:13 - For great [is] thy mercy toward me: and thou hast delivered my soul from the lowest hell.* In *John 14:2-3*, Jesus said: *"In my Father's house are many mansions: if it were not so, I would have told you. I go to prepare a place for you, and if I go and prepare a place for you, I will come again and receive you unto myself; that where I am, there ye may be also."*
- ➢ We are redeemed from the law, and justified through faith: *Galatians 4:5- To redeem them that were under the law, that we might receive the adoption of sons.*
- ➢ We were redeemed from our enemies, and given victory in Christ Jesus:
  Jeremiah 15:21 - And I will deliver thee out of the hand of the wicked, and I will redeem thee out of the hand of the terrible.

Because mankind was responsible for his own sins, it was he who was under obligation to pay the supreme penalty-his life. Mankind (beginning with Adam and Eve) had made a covenant with death. Yet we know that God's covenant through Jesus was far better. Through Jesus' death and resurrection, we were released from captivity. Our minds were held by Satan and by our own inability to free ourselves. Jesus paid a precious price that was a sweet-smelling savor to God. Because of what Jesus did, we are justified (made right) with God. Now we are free to live out the holy calling that God has placed on our lives.

Therefore, we should know that we have always been of value to God. He has always known us. He said so through the apostle Paul:

> "But God, who is rich in mercy, because of His great love with which He loved us, even when we were dead in trespasses, made us alive together with Christ ... that in the ages to come He might show the exceeding riches of His grace in His kindness toward us in Christ Jesus" (Ephesians 2:4-7).

Jesus gave His life and paid the supreme penalty in exchange for something of great value to God-us. His act of mercy and grace did not go unnoticed. God honored His Son Jesus:

> "Wherefore God also hath highly exalted him, and given him a name which is above every name: That at the name of Jesus every knee should bow, of things in heaven, and things in earth, and things under the earth; And that every tongue should confess that Jesus Christ is Lord, to the glory of God the Father" (Philippians 2:9-11).

Thank God for Jesus!

> **Affirmation # 9: You have always been of value to God; that is why He bought you with a very precious price, even the best that He could give-the death of His only Son-Jesus.**
>
> *"For God so loved the world, that he gave his only begotten Son, that whosoever believeth in him should not perish, but have everlasting life." John 3:16.*
>
> *For ye are bought with a price: therefore glorify God in your body, and in your spirit, which are God's.*
>
> *1 Corinthians 6:20*

Your assignment: In your journal, write a prayer to God thanking Him for how He redeemed you through the gift He gave to you-His Son Jesus Christ.

Journal   Date_____

CHAPTER 11

"In Christ Jesus, You are Never Alone"

"Fear thou not; for I am with thee: be not dismayed; for I am thy God: I will strengthen thee; yea, I will help thee; yea, I will uphold thee with the right hand of my righteousness. (Isaiah 41:10).

Throughout the Bible, God confirms that we are not alone. One of the ways that He gets this poignant message to us is by using other Bible saints to show us through vicarious experiences, examples of His abiding presence.

Joshua, the son of Nun and successor to Moses can attest to this. For years, Joshua had been Moses' faithful assistant. He had watched as Moses led the Israelites through the Red Sea. He was one of the twelve scouts that Moses sent to spy out the land of Canaan. In fact, because of the positive report that he and Caleb brought back from the "promised land", he along with Caleb would be the only two faithful men who came out of slavery in Egypt, and were allowed to enter it.

Before Moses' impending death, God charged him to lay his hands on Joshua as his successor. Joshua, though saddened by the revelation that his mentor was about to die, must have thought of the awesome task that was before him. He would be responsible for leading at least two million of God's people into Canaan.

After Moses' death, God knew the awesomeness of the responsibility Joshua was to face, as evidenced by the words He spoke to him:

> "Moses my servant is dead; now therefore arise, go over this Jordan, thou and all this people, unto the land which I do give to them, even to the children of Israel... There shall not any man be able to stand before thee all the days of thy life: as I was with Moses, so I will be with thee: I will not fail thee, nor forsake thee. Be strong and of a good courage: for unto this people shalt thou divide for an inheritance the land, which I sware unto their fathers to give them. Only be thou strong and very courageous, that thou mayest observe to do according to all the law, which Moses my servant commanded thee: turn not from it to the right hand or to the left that thou mayest prosper whithersoever thou goest. This book of the law shall not depart out of thy mouth; but thou shall meditate therein day and night; that thou mayest observe to do according to all that is written therein; for then thou shalt make thy way prosperous, and then thou shalt have good success. Have not I commanded thee? Be strong and of a good courage; be not afraid, neither be thou dismayed; for the Lord thy God is with thee whithersoever thou goest" (Joshua 1:2; 1:5-9).

What an awesome promise from an almighty God! More than once in this passage, He exhorted Joshua to "be strong and of a good courage". Notice that with this comforting, confident assurance from

God, Joshua knew that he could and would not fail, and began to *immediately* command the people. This account demonstrates that not only does God tell us that we are not alone; He exhorts us to take courage and act because He himself is there with us wherever we go.

Another great example of God's assurance that He will forever be with us is intertwined in the story of the Prophet Elijah. He was a prophet during the reign of King Ahab and his evil wife Jezebel.

Elijah confronted King Ahab and the people of Israel regarding their cultic worship of the idol, Baal. Elijah commanded King Ahab to assemble the nation of Israel along with the 450 prophets of Baal, and the 400 prophets who sacrificed in the high places, and were taken care of by Jezebel, to Mount Carmel for a holy showdown. As the crowd assembled, Elijah raised this thought- provoking question:

"How long halt ye between two opinions? If the Lord be God, follow him; but if Baal, then follow him. And the people answered him not a word" (1 Kings 18:21).

Elijah gave the false prophets orders to dismember and lay their sacrifice on the altar of Baal. While he prepared the second bullock, they were to call upon Baal to consume their sacrifice with fire. They called from morning until the time of the evening sacrifice. Nothing happened. They even cut themselves so that blood streamed from their wounds. No Baal.

Now it was Elijah's turn. He built an altar to the Lord with twelve stones representing each tribe of Israel. Those assembled looked on with shock as he made a trench around the altar, and prepared the meat and the wood for sacrifice. Imagine their astonishment when Elijah ordered them of pour water on the sacrifice and on the wood, not once, but three times! "Elijah must be delusional. Everybody knows that fire and water does not mix. Surely he's making it impossible for this sacrifice to burn," they may have thought. Then Elijah prayed to the God of heaven and earth:

"And it came to pass at the time of the offering of the evening sacrifice, that Elijah the prophet came near, and said, Lord God of Abraham, Isaac, and of Israel, let it be known this day that thou art God in Israel, and that I am thy servant, and that I have done all these things at thy word. Hear me, O Lord, hear me, that this people may know that thou art the Lord God, and that thou hast turned their heart back again" (1 Kings 18:36-37).

Elijah knew the power of God. He was aware that it did not take God long to show Himself strong:

"Then the fire of the Lord fell, and consumed the burnt sacrifice, and the wood, and the stones, and the dust, and licked up the water that was in the trench. And when all the people saw it, they fell on their faces and they said, "The Lord, he is the God; the Lord, he is the God. And Elijah said unto them, take the prophets of Baal; let not one of them escape. And they took them: and Elijah brought them down to the brook Kishon, and slew them there." (1 Kings 18:38-40).

It did not take long for the news of the day's events to get to the ears of Queen Jezebel. Wimpy King Ahab told his wife everything that Elijah had done. Conniving, controlling Jezebel was furious. She sent Elijah a message stating her intent to kill him by the end of the next day.

Thus, soon after his victory over the prophets of Baal on Mount Carmel, Elijah finds himself running scared for his life. What has led to this turn-about in the life of a man who was so obedient to God? It is fear brought on by the wrath of an evil woman. Frightened, seemingly alone and discouraged, Elijah runs, and keeps on running. He hasn't stopped to hear a word from the Lord. He has quickly forgotten God's power in the amazing feat that was just performed through him in the midst of the people of Israel. He is now afraid of the words of a vicious, revenge-seeking queen.

Even though God's power is evident, Elijah notices that no one has come to his aid. Not one has come out of the crowd after so strong a display. Not one has declared: *"For God I will live and for God I will die."* No one comes to greet him and say, *"Elijah, I'll stand with you."* He is seemingly alone. Elijah's despair leads him to run far away and deep into the utter recesses of a cave. Oftentimes, in our distress, our fear of eminent danger can cause us to run and hide from our enemies, and even try to hide from God.

Elijah's life also shows us that God will reveal Himself to us in times of trouble, though not in the manner that we expect. Now that Elijah has taken the time to settle down, the Lord speaks to him: *"What doest thou here, Elijah."* *(1 Kings 19:9d).* Elijah quickly explains as if God does not already know. Then, God commands Elijah to go to the mouth of the cave to meet with Him:

> *"And he said, Go forth, and stand upon the mount before the Lord. And, behold the Lord passed by, and a great and strong wind rent the mountains, and brake in pieces the rocks before the Lord; but the Lord was not in the wind: and after the wind an earthquake, but the Lord was not in the earthquake: And after the earthquake, a fire; but the Lord was not in the fire: and after the fire a still small voice. And it was so that when Elijah heard it, that he wrapped his face in his mantle, and went out, and stood in the entering in of the cave. And, behold, there came a voice unto him, and said, What doest thou here, Elijah?"* *(1 Kings 19:11-13).*

Child of God, like Elijah, we are often fearful of the words and perceived actions of people. We base our lives on what others will think of us. Also, we expect God to show Himself to us in some spectacular, grandiose way. All the while, He is whispering to us in that still, small voice that says, *"Though you may feel as if you are alone in your trials; though you may feel that you are afraid to be obedient to my calling, I am with you. Trust me. You will never be alone. Realize also that I still have thousands who have not bowed their heads to some other god, but have given their allegiance wholly to me. Son/daughter of God, the greatest testimony you can have is to believe my word."*

Now God has Elijah's undivided attention. He then tells Elijah what he must do. After God speaks (1 Kings 19:15-18), Elijah realizes that his earthly mission has come to an end. He then leaves the cave and follows the directions of the Lord.

God wants us to know that when situations arise that seem out of our control, we are never alone. He made this truth clear to Joshua and Elijah. Through their experiences and through studying other passages in His word, He makes it clear to us. Listen to the words of Jesus as He speaks to His disciples (and us) in John 14:14-18):

> *"If ye love me, keep my commandments. And I will pray the Father, and He shall give you another Comforter, that He may abide with you forever; even the Spirit of truth; whom the world cannot receive, because it seeth him not, neither knoweth him; but ye know him, for he dwelleth with you, and shall be in you. I will not leave you comfortless; I will come to you."* (Underlined emphasis is mine).

What a promise! Jesus did not want us to be alone, or ever think that we were. He knew that we would need somebody to help us along in our Christian walk. He knew that we would encounter many persecutions, trials and perils in this life. He therefore petitioned the Father on our behalf to send us a *Comforter* in the person of the *Holy Spirit*. God sent someone to teach us, to guide us, to advise us, to comfort us during our darkest hours-during those times when it seemed as if midnight would last forever, and daylight was so far away. He sent someone to us when we felt that we had no more tears left to cry. God sent someone to pray for us when we did not have the strength to pray for ourselves. That *someone* was in the person of the Holy Spirit. To make it even more "up close and personal" the Holy Spirit has taken residence within us. Where we go, He goes. So as you can see, you are never alone. Even in the heat of battle, you're not alone. The Holy Spirit lives in you. *What a mighty God we serve!*

Affirmation # 10 God has not nor will He ever leave you to bear any situation alone.

"There hath no temptation taken you but such as is common to man: but God [is] faithful, who will not suffer you to be tempted above that ye are able; but will with the temptation also make a way to escape, that ye may be able to bear [it]." 1 Corinthians 10:13;

"Go ye therefore, and teach all nations, baptizing them in the name of the Father, and of the Son, and of the Holy Ghost: Teaching them to observe all things whatsoever I have commanded you: and, lo, I am with you alway, [even] unto the end of the world. Amen". Matthew 28:10-20

"Let your conversation be without covetousness; and be content with such things as ye have: for he hath said, I will never leave thee, nor forsake thee." Hebrews 13:5.

"And I will pray the Father, and he shall give you another Comforter, that he may abide with you for ever; Even the Spirit of truth; whom the world cannot receive, because it seeth him not, neither knoweth him: but ye know him; for he dwelleth with you, and shall be in you. I will not leave you comfortless: I will come to you." John 14:16-18

Your Assignment:

Do not allow the words "of the world" to make you fearful nor dictate who you are in Christ Jesus. Your only standard of reference is the word of God. When facing a difficult situation, ask yourself these questions:

> ➤ What does God say about the situation that I am now facing?
> ➤ Are there recorded life experiences of saints (or non-saints) from which I can learn?

Your assignment: Study your bible. Then answer the following questions in your journal: What does God say about sickness, healing, health, sin, long life, and poverty?

Journal   Date_____

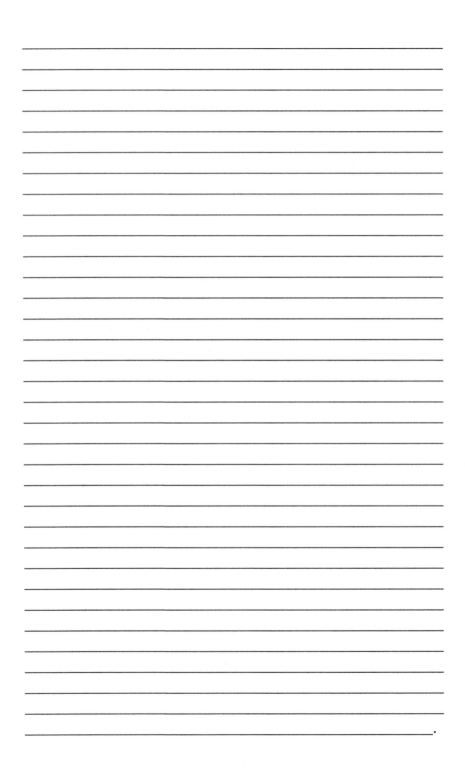

A WORD OF ENCOURAGEMENT FROM THE AUTHOR

The only life you have in this physical world is the life that you have before you. Yes, the one that you are living now. You cannot live in the past; neither can you change the things that have happened in the past. You must live in the *"Now"*. Sure, you've been hurt. Sure, you've been disappointed. Sure, you've done things that you wish that you had not done. Who hasn't? The scriptures say that *"all have sinned and fall short of the glory of God"(Romans 3:23).* If you feel guilty and discouraged because of things that have happened *"back in the day,"* then child of God, you must seek God. Go to Him and prayerfully ask for His forgiveness and restoration. He won't disappoint you: *"If we confess our sins, he is faithful and just to forgive us [our] sins, and to cleanse us from all unrighteousness", (1 John 1:9).*

Remember also that God has left you the precious gift of His word. It's His own personal letter to you. Through His word, He says to you just as He said to Jeremiah the prophet: *"Before I formed thee in the belly I knew thee; and before thou camest forth out of the womb I sanctified thee, and I ordained thee a prophet unto the nations" (Jeremiah 1:5).*

He already knew what you would have to face, and He left you a letter to help you learn of Him. All you need to do, is to read (He will give you the wisdom and understanding that you need) and obey.

Now, without murmuring or complaining about what could have been, press on: *"I press toward the mark for the prize of the high calling of God in Christ Jesus" Philippians 3:14)*. Think of the minute that you're in right now, then, move on into the present. Your future is not *"back there"* it is ahead of you. It has already been planned:

> *"For I know the plans I have for you," declares the Lord, "plans to prosper you and not to harm you, plans to give you hope and a future." (Jeremiah 29:11).*

You're alive! *So live!* God has quickened you with all that you need to be successful in this life. Use what you already have in your hand-the gifts that God has given you! Continue to thank God for sending His Son Jesus to die in your place. Then, worship, honor and praise Him with your mouth:

"By him therefore let us offer the sacrifice of praise to God continually, that is, the fruit of our lips giving thanks to his name" (Hebrews 13:15).

Show Him that you are grateful by obeying His word:

> *"And Samuel said, Hath the LORD as great delight in burnt offerings and sacrifices, as in obeying the voice of the LORD? Behold, to obey is better than sacrifice, and to hearken than the fat of rams". (I Samuel 15:22).*

Know that *"it is in Him that you live, and move, and have your being" (Acts 17:28), and "Be thankful unto Him and bless His name" (Psalm 100:5).* He's already blessed yours.

Now, go on. You may take baby steps at first, but you must "Go forth and live" the life that He has called you to live *"In Christ Jesus".* Tell His story to the world. You are more than "filthy rags. Be who God has called you to be.

AN INVITATION

If you have not accepted Jesus as your Savior, it would be inappropriate and downright sinful if I did not offer you the chance to know Him. God is a loving, kind and caring God *("He careth for you"* 1 Peter 5:7). He is not like anyone or anything I've ever experienced; and He can be the same for you. When no one else will listen or seek to understand, when the world and even those closest to you seem not to offer support, God is right there to give an ear to your every cry. He will hold you in His arms. He will protect you and keep you in the shadow of His wings:

> *"Be merciful unto me, O God, be merciful unto me: for my soul trusteth in thee: yea, in the shadow of thy wings will I make my refuge, until these calamities be overpast" (Psalm 57:1).*

God will guide you, and teach you, and yes, He will chastise you for your own good: *"For whom the Lord loveth he chasteneth, and scourgeth every son whom he receiveth." (Hebrews 12:6).* Admit it. You would not want a God who would allow you to get away with sin.

I love Him and want you to know Him too. It is not by accident that you have picked up this book. If you do not know Jesus as your personal Savior, now is your chance. He is patiently waiting for you to call upon His name. His word says:

"Neither is there salvation in any other: for there is none other name under heaven given among men, whereby we must be saved" (Acts 4:12). That name is JESUS.

I invite you to pray this prayer (or one of your own) with me:

"Lord Jesus, I acknowledge that I am a sinner because there is nothing that I can hide from you. I am sorry for the sins that I have committed against You and others, and ask that you forgive me and come into my heart. I pledge to turn away from the wrong that I have done, and turn to you for guidance in every area of my life. I believe that you died for my sins and were raised from the dead. I accept Your sacrifice, and I ask you to accept me as one of Your children. Lord, teach me Your ways. Thank you for eternal life through your Son Jesus Christ. Amen.

Now find a bible-believing, bible teaching church so that you can develop a healthy relationship with God and with other saints. It is also vitally imperative that you begin to read and study your bible and be obedient to what it says.

My sister, my brother, you have made the best decision you will ever make in this life and in the life to come.

Welcome to the family of God!

BIBLIOGRAPHY

1. Easton, M. G. *Illustrated Bible Dictionary.* Thomas A. Nelson Publishers, 1897. Available: ***http://cf.blueletterbible.org***.
2. Kirkwood, David. *The Christian Disciple's Manual: Life-Changing Truths for Every Believer.* Pittsburgh, Pennsylvania: ETHNOS, 1992.
3. *Merriam Webster Online Dictionary (2007).* Springfield, Massachusetts: Merriam Webster, Inc. Available: ***http://www.m-w.com/***.
4. *Orr, James. International Standard Bible Encyclopedia (1915). "Covenant of Salt". Available: **http://www.studylight.org** and **http://cf.blueletterbible.org**.*
5. Stanley, Charles (2003, December 16) "The God Who Rescues Us" (Daily Devotional) *IN TOUCH Magazine.* Available at ***www.intouchministries.org***.
6. Warren, Rick. *The Purpose Driven Life: What on Earth Am I Here For?* Grand Rapids, Michigan: Zondervan, 2002.
7. ***WebBibleEncyclopeida@ChristianAnswers.net***.

Printed in the United States
By Bookmasters